61-18073

5-2-62

The Middle West

The Middle West

A Study of Progress

SIDNEY GLAZER
Wayne State University

BOOKMAN ASSOCIATES :: New York

MANUFACTURED IN THE UNITED STATES OF AMERICA BY
UNITED PRINTING SERVICES, INC.
NEW HAVEN, CONN.

A HISTORICAL SURVEY DETAILING THE
ECONOMIC, POLITICAL, AND SOCIAL
CONDITIONS THAT MADE FOR THE PHE-
NOMENAL GROWTH OF THE MIDWEST.

Preface

This book is designed to tell a portion of the great story of the Middle West. A complete regional history, of course, would require many volumes. The area is one in which we can find the farm, the factory, and the tourist retreat. Its social, ethnic, and religious strains are numerous. In any one of its states the electorate may choose a Democrat for governor and send, at the same time, a Republican to the Senate.

I have been guided, in part, in organizing the pattern of my book by the questions of students in my classes in the History of the Middle West. Professor Joe Norris, my colleague in the History Department, has given informal counsel on a number of occasions. I am especially indebted to Professor Alex Brede of the English Department who has read parts of the manuscript and made most helpful suggestions.

Contents

Contents

The Middle West

Historical Survey

U NLIKE some of our regions, the Middle West lacks precise boundaries. Apparently to many, the term is a mere vague geographic phenomenon embracing the vast area somewhere between two great mountain chains —the Alleghenies and the Rockies. To others it is synonymous with the old Northwest, which comprises Ohio, Indiana, Illinois, Michigan and Wisconsin. Many regard it as a somewhat indefinite region with fluid boundaries, centering around the upper Mississippi Valley and sharing common political and economic interests.

But, the designation "Middle West" is accepted without question. As used in this book the "Middle West" designates the region encompassing the states of the old Northwest and Iowa, Minnesota, Kansas, Nebraska, North Dakota, and South Dakota. Obviously, except for the accident of state boundaries, the border towns on the periphery, properly could be, and indeed often are, regarded as a part of the area.

Although the differences between the states are numerous, they are not sharp enough to bring divisions. Furthermore, the many similarities, which are the product of a large number of forces, are more numerous and basic than the differences.

13

Historical tradition has played an important role in determining the character of the Middle West. The agrarian settlement of the Middle West began at a time when the tradition of American nationality was strong except, possibly, in a few areas in the South.

In spite of the understandable local pride and local loyalties, the people of the Middle West lacked any intense regional feeling. By 1860 the majority of the inhabitants of the Middle West believed that the United States was one strong and indissoluble nation. This belief in the Federal government was strengthened as the Congress undertook policies favorable to the region.

The institutional pattern of the region was nineteenth-century in orientation. Although it was settled by men and women from many levels of society, a relatively high degree of equalitarianism prevailed. This spirit gave rise to a very effective democracy.

The flow of immigration into the Middle West, native and foreign born, has been almost continuous. Each decade of spectacular population growth brought new vitality. Each new population element made its characteristic contribution to the building of the arts.

Geographic factors have been highly significant in shaping the development of the Middle West. Midwesterners are aware that some of their good fortune is the result of a favorable geographic situation and an abundance of physical resources. Nature has been unusually kind to the Middle West, which possesses so many of the materials essential for a modern industrial age.

Although there are climatic differences within the Middle West, only a relatively small portion of the region is sufficiently unattractive to bar profitable economic activities. In turn, these climatic differences have both encompassed and made possible a wide variety of industries. They also were the basis of the earlier agricultural specialization. In the long run, this climatic diversity has enormously aided the enterprises of the area.

The Middle West contained millions of acres of fertile land, which at the time of the coming of the first settlers, had never been ploughed. This good land was the greatest of all the natural resources of the region. Much of the land, while awaiting the first stages of preparation, immediately afforded at least a minimum standard of living. The daring pioneers found it possible to subsist with a reasonable degree of comfort upon the gifts of nature. This rich land was well distributed. The many productive farms furnish much of the food for the fast-growing population of the nation. Yet, at the same time, the region exports a large volume of food to many nations.

The waterways are among the major assets of the Middle West. In the early years of settlement these waterways were the major, and, most frequently, the sole means of transportation. The Great Lakes afforded transportation for the French explorers, and now serve as major arteries of transportation in our modern industrial society. They have made possible, for example, the giant steel industry which mixes ore in the Lake Superior region and smelts it in Indiana and Ohio and Pennsylvania. The Upper Mississippi system was likewise largely significant. With few exceptions the rivers were navigable and helped to determine the location of the first settlements.

The region possesses a vast store of useful and valuable minerals. The rich iron deposits of the Lake Superior region have been the chief domestic source of supply. Much of the copper mined in the Middle West has come from the rich lodes of Michigan's Upper Peninsula. The Calumet and Hecla, made possible by eastern capital, was the greatest of the mining companies active in Michigan.

Rich coal deposits are found in many of the states. The mining of coal, however, has been of major economic significance only in Ohio, Illinois, and Indiana. The reserves in these and other states are large.

The production of salt is of especial importance in Michigan. Large reserves of petroleum have been found in Kansas and North Dakota. The petroleum industry, however, is far from insignificant in several of the other states.

In many areas the heavy forests found by the pioneers helped to assure survival. Often the extensiveness of timber land was regarded as an impediment to agriculture. By the middle of the nineteenth century, however, the great lumbering town was already under way in Michigan and Wisconsin.

The extent of the fertile land and the abundance of mineral and forest resources suggested, almost from the beginning of American settlement in the Middle West, the great future economic advances. The almost continuous availability of land inspired pioneers with a hope of individual wealth and produced an agrarianism which was dominant in the region's life until years after the Civil War. The widespread ownership of land gave rise to a powerful and general spirit of independence. The very task of overcoming barriers encouraged the region's historically famous confidence and optimism.

Natural resources, even impressive statistics of resources, do not quite tell the story of the Middle West. Fundamentally the Middle West is people. They gave the region its character and culture. They shaped the history. This history goes back to the time of the early explorers.

Throughout much of the Middle West, the first European explorers and settlers were French. In 1615, Samuel Champlain, the founder of New France, reached the Georgian Bay area at the northern end of Lake Huron. Within a decade one of his protégés, Etienne Brulé, after extensive exploration in the Lake Huron region, had skirted the southern shores of Lake Superior and reached a point westward as far as present-day Duluth.

The youthful Brulé was but the first of many famous explorers to penetrate an unknown, and sometimes perilous, wilderness. In 1634 Jean Nicolet left the Georgian Bay country and passed through the Straits of Mackinac on a journey that he hoped would bring him immortality as the discover of a new and short route to the Far East. He soon reached the Green Bay Peninsula only to discover that his dreams of Asiatic treasures would never be fulfilled. Although his report brought some disappointment, the French at least became better aware of the immensity of the area they were exploring.

Champlain was interested in missionary activities and the betterment of the natives. In 1615 he invited the Recollect Order to send missionaries to the New World. Later, Jesuits supplemented the Recollects. The missionaries, temperate and understanding men, filled their roles competently and acquired prestige among the natives. In the face of spectacular hardships, they brought their religion and some inkling of the pattern of a new civilization to the natives. They helped the Indian to acquire some of the skills previously unknown in the New World and, on occasion, apparently gave some elementary instruction in academic subjects.

In the second half of the seventeenth century, Father Marquette, Louis Jolliet, and Robert Cavelier LaSalle achieved great fame among the host of major explorers. By the close of the seventeenth century the French had acquired, largely through discovery, control of the Great Mississippi Valley. New France extended from the mouth of the St. Lawrence to the mouth of the Mississippi.

The lucrative fur trade was the chief stimulus for this

great French expansion. Officially this trade was organized on a monopolistic basis. In practice, almost all of the French could engage in some form of this highly profitable occupation. This included even the men who virtually deserted the civilization of the White Man to live among the Indians.

By the middle of the eighteenth century the French had established a number of key posts. Ordinarily these served as combined military, commercial, and missionary centers. By far the most important of these was Detroit, founded in 1701, by Antoine de la Mothe Cadillac. The lesser communities, however, were numerous. Green Bay, La Crosse, and Vincennes are but three among many Midwestern cities of contemporary importance whose origins can be traced to this French era.

Between 1689 and 1763 France and England engaged, intermittently, in four wars that had their North American colonial accompaniments. The Seven Years War, 1756-1763, known to the colonists as the French and Indian War, was the fourth major European conflict involving England and France during the colonial era. In this conflict the very existence of England was at stake. The British decided to strike at the entire French Empire.

The American colonists gave an unstinting support in men and money to their Mother Country. They fought courageously to remove French influence from this continent. In 1760, Montreal, the last of the eastern French defenses, had fallen to the English.

In 1760, the capture of Detroit by the Rogers Rangers, under the command of Robert Rogers, hero of Kenneth Robert's famous novel *Northwest Passage,* led to the French loss of the Great Lakes country.

In 1763 the French and their allies accepted the humiliating terms of a treaty whereby France was forced to cede all except the bare remnants of a once vast empire to the victor.

The subsequent influences of the French regime in the area were not great. Self-rule was never fostered because of the French policy of reducing subjects to a state of virtual complete dependence. Nevertheless, the process of establishing the initial settlements is always difficult. The groundwork laid by the French aided later settlers in so many respects. Likewise, the French had, for the most part, secured the friendship of the Indians and accustomed them to the white men and their ways. Significantly too, some twenty thousand French inhabitants of the later Middle West constituted a highly desirable foundation upon which to build the future cultures.

The English were not total strangers to the newly acquired country. Early in the eighteenth century, English traders had started their penetration of the Upper Ohio country. The English, because of an absence of governmental restrictions, could compete favorably for the very profitable Indian trade. The early traders helped, also, to undermine the informal French understanding with the Indians. By 1730 the English commercial sphere reached even to the remote Wabash Valley.

Land speculators also recognized the desirability of the Ohio region. In 1747 Virginian and English speculators formed the Ohio Company, the first of several companies to bear this name. In 1748 this company was given a tentative and conditional grant of 500,000 acres by the English government. The hopes of the company were premature and nebulous. Nevertheless, the grant stimulated an interest in the Ohio country.

In many respects, in 1763, conditions seemed favorable for significant English settlement in the West. Two barriers, however, both unforeseen, immediately retarded this migration. The first was the Pontiac conspiracy. This is the name given to the large-scale Indian warfare directed against all of the newly acquired British posts. The colorful Ottawa chieftain, Pontiac, hoped that the military strength of his informal confederation would impress the British. Although some garrisons were destroyed, Pontiac was forced ultimately to ask the British for terms of peace. The conspiracy called attention, however, to the question of possible hostile Indian reaction to settlement.

The second barrier was perhaps the more formidable. In 1763 the British by an edict, known as the Proclamation of 1763, virtually barred American settlement beyond the Appalachians. It is now known that the English intended this prohibition to be temporary. Their administrators believed that the Indian question and conflicting colonial land claims, among other major problems, could best be solved by this restriction of immigration.

These restrictive policies did not entirely bar migration to the West. In 1763, shrewd Americans realized that the westward movement had reached the Alleghenies. Many men were ready to take their families beyond the mountains into the Ohio Valley. Land speculators were equally anxious to see the West develop. Occasionally the terms of the Proclamation were relaxed. Nevertheless, transportation difficulties, the fear of Indians, and lack of specific knowledge about the soil reduced the number of newcomers north of the Ohio to an insignificant trickle.

In 1774, under the terms of the Quebec Act, the area north of the Ohio River was awarded to Quebec. For practical purposes this measure suggested that the region would, when settled, acquire a French culture. The English colonists were so aroused over this proposal that they included the decree among the Intolerable Acts contributing to the immediate outbreak of the American Revolution.

In the early years of the American Revolution the West was firmly in the grip of the English. This control was challenged by the young Virginian, George Rogers Clark, who, acting with the approval of his own state and the Continental Congress, led a small force westward to win the Ohio country from the English. In the heroic campaign of 1777-1778 Clark wrested the posts as far west as the Mississippi River and as far north as Vincennes. This victory helped to establish the American claim for the western country.

By the terms of the Treaty of Paris, 1783, closing the American Revolution, the new United States acquired the land—with the exception of Florida—west of the Mississippi and south of Canada. The English, however, refused to surrender Detroit and other posts on the Great Lakes on the grounds that the Americans had not compensated the Loyalists. After years of negotiations, the region, in accordance with the terms of the Jay Treaty, was finally surrendered in 1796.

During the Revolution, the individual states again acquired a complete control over the unassigned western lands. However, the states, in turn, were forced to cede their western claims to the new central government, the Articles of Confederation, in order to secure ratification. Only by this arrangement were the smaller states satisfied that they could attain a genuine equality.

In 1784 Congress seriously studied the problem of the frontier. In a report known as the Ordinance of 1784, the great Thomas Jefferson outlined a plan of government for the entire West, North and South, in which he proposed complete political rights for all of the settlers by the ultimate creation of as many as sixteen states. This classical scholar had already selected Greek names, such as Metropolania and Polypotamia, that would embody the basic geographic characteristics of each area. Temporary governments were to be established in each until the population reached 20,000, at which time each would become eligible for statehood on a basis of equality with the original thirteen. Jefferson's proposal also included certain guarantees of civil rights and an explicit prohibition of slavery. This most intelligent ordinance actually was enacted on April 2, 1784, but technicalities forced it to remain inoperative.

Although many members of the Congress were willing enough to delay the formulation of a plan of government for the West, this postponement of land sales was depriving the government of revenues. The Ordinance of 1785 was the congressional response to the problem of land distribution. With some small exceptions, this ordinance authorized the survey of land west of Pennsylvania. The Ordinance provided that the township of thirty-six square miles bound on meridians of longitude and parallels of latitude, was to be the unit of survey. Each of the square miles of 640 acres was known as a section. One section in each township was to be reserved for the support of education. One half of the townships was to be sold in entirety, presumably to speculators, and the other half in sections to the individual farmers. The minimum price was one dollar an acre to be sold at auctions. The plan of a rectangular township appealed to New Englanders, who visualized the establishment of many compact communities with the township as the basic unit.

Even at the minimum price of $640, few could purchase from the government. Congress also made large grants to land companies who received their tracts, in effect, at reduced rates. Several companies formulated ambitious plans for the settlement of large areas in the northern Ohio Valley. Obviously, these companies could not hope to attract any significant number of settlers until a future form of democratic government was assured. In 1786, at the Bunch of Grapes Tavern in Boston, a group of investors, largely New Englanders, formed the Ohio Company, and selected the

Reverend Manassah Cutler as a spokesman to press Congress for the establishment of a plan of government.

Congress responded most intelligently with the famous Northwest Ordinance of 1787. This measure created the Northwest Territory for the area north of the Ohio and east of the Mississippi with the pledge of the ultimate establishment of not less than three nor more than five states. Ultimately the five states of Ohio, Indiana, Illinois, Michigan and Wisconsin were carved out of this vast area—familiarly known as the Old Northwest.

The officials of this temporary government were to be an appointed governor, three judges, and a secretary. When a population of five thousand males of voting age was attained, a legislature was to be set up. The territory was to be eligible for statehood when it reached a population of sixty thousand. This creation of a territory—so explicitly not a colony—with its varying dependence upon the central government to assure the adequate preparation for statehood, was a most remarkable contribution of the Articles of Confederation. This general plan of government was accompanied by equally unusual and equally intelligent provisions guaranteeing such basic rights as trial by jury. Congress took positive steps to assure freedom of religion and thus to promote the necessary minimum of morality on which any stable government must rest. To the same end it encouraged the beginnings of a school system.

The Ordinance of 1787 provided for graduated steps of territorial self-government in proportion to the increase in population. Personal liberty, freedom of religion, free and public education, the exclusion of slavery, and the recognition of federal supremacy were assured by the Ordinance. The policies formulated in 1787 essentially influenced the basic attitudes, policies and institutions of the later states.

The Ordinance of 1787 met the requirements of Cutler

and his associates who acquired the title to 1,500,000 acres on the Ohio and Muskingum Rivers. Agents were immediately sent to the West to pave the way for settlers. On April 7, 1788 the first band of settlers founded Marietta, Ohio, the forerunner of many thriving communities to be found in the region.

Marietta had capable leadership. The majority of the first settlers were New Englanders, many of whom had served in the Revolution. These men helped to introduce New England institutions in the new country. The cultural foundations were characteristically laid with the establishment of a school in 1789, just one year after the official founding. Marietta College was, in turn, founded in 1797.

A second company also played an important role in initiation of organized settlement in the Old Northwest. The Symmes Company, founded by John Clever Symmes, of New Jersey, secured a large tract near the mouth of the Miami. In 1788 the company founded Cincinnati. The interests of many of the settlers from the Middle Atlantic States left their imprint upon the city which rapidly rose as the first metropolis of the Ohio Valley.

The city of Gallipolis was given its unique name by French settlers, many of whom were middle-class refugees of the Revolution. These unfortunate people had migrated to America under the assumption that they could lead a middle-class life in the wilderness. A majority of these immigrants arrived in the New World almost penniless only to discover the misrepresentations made to them by a land company, the Sciota, whose grandiose plans never materialized for lack of capital. Sympathetic members of Congress gave them land on the Ohio. A small band then went to the new country and founded Gallipolis. Ohio acquired at least a slight Virginian flavor of society when many veterans of the Revolution settled on the Virginia Reserve, which Virginia had retained for its veterans.

The initial settlement of northwestern Ohio also began late in the eighteenth century. The Connecticut Land Company had acquired huge tracts from the state of Connecticut which had retained this land in northwestern Ohio, known as the Western Reserve, to aid its veterans. In 1796 Moses Cleaveland, an agent for the company, made his headquarters in a village which was to bear his name (the spelling was later changed to the present form of Cleveland). The majority of the immigrants to the Western Reserve country reached their new homes by way of the Genessee Road, which extended from western New York.

Indian hostilities, of course, posed an immediate problem. Many Indians of the Northwest refused to honor the jurisdiction of the American government. The Indians inflicted defeats upon General Jacob Harmar and Arthur St. Clair, the governor of the Northwest Territory. President Washington then directed General Anthony Wayne, known to later generations as "Mad Anthony," to undertake a large-scale campaign against the Indians. Wayne skillfully trained his force for specialized Indian warfare, and although he often employed unorthodox methods, he defeated the Indians at the Battle of Fallen Timbers near present-day Toledo. The subsequent treaty of Greenville—now Greenville, Ohio—in 1795 relieved prospective settlers of an immediate fear, since the Indians recognized the political jurisdiction of the new American government over the Northwest.

In 1800 the future state of Ohio had a population of 45,000. Two years later Congress approved an enabling act providing for the election of members to a constitutional convention. This convention drafted the first constitution for Ohio which became a state on March 1, 1803. Statehood served as a major stimulus for further growth. In 1810 Ohio could boast of a population of 232,000.

The War of 1812 temporarily retarded settlement. The Western communities correctly recognized the dual character of the war as a struggle with England and also as a struggle with Indians who were allied with the British, primarily to hinder further American settlement. The surrender of Detroit to the English, early in 1812, brought real alarm to the entire Middle West. The British successes, and the strength of their alliances with the Indians, greatly angered the inhabitants of the Midwestern communities who gave their loyal support to the war effort.

Early in 1813 an American force, which included a large contingent from the Ohio militia, was virtually massacred at Frenchtown, now known as Monroe, Michigan. This defeat seemed to indicate little hope of regaining Detroit without control of Lake Erie. In 1813 the victory of Commodore Perry at Put-in-Bay on Lake Erie doomed English rule over Detroit. The British were forced to withdraw from the city. As a result, during the remaining months of the war, Americans throughout the entire Northwest enjoyed a new security.

The first eastern settlers in the Ohio Valley ordinarily made their way to Pittsburgh. Then the emigrants usually traveled on a river boat from Pittsburgh to the towns of the Ohio River still further west. This same route was a principal artery of transportation for later settlers who took up land in Indiana and Illinois.

After the War of 1812 the flow of migration to the Old Northwest assumed new proportions. The accounts of rich farm lands were publicized throughout the entire East. Many of the veterans of the war sought new homes in the West. Between 1810 and 1820 the population of Ohio swelled to 581,000. Indiana, which had attained statehood in 1816, had a population of 147,000. Illinois, admitted to the Union two years after Indiana became a state, also had a population of 147,000.

Settlement in Indiana before 1812 was painfully slow. Some newcomers moved to Vincennes and other communities founded by the French. A few towns were established on the Ohio. The immigrants who came after the war tended to cluster in the southern portions of Indiana. The settlers included a large number of Kentuckians who scoured the hills in search of new and better lands.

In many respects the settlement of Illinois was parallel to that of Indiana. The first new towns to come into existence were river towns. Until 1825 a large number of the newcomers were of a southern background. After the completion of the Erie Canal in 1825, immigrants from New England and western New York moved in large numbers to the rich lands of the state.

Many of the Illinois settlers made new homes in the prairies so ably described by the observant English traveler, Charles Joseph Latrobe.

> They the prairies do not resemble the wide levels of France, the high lands of Spain, or the rich plains of Italy;— as, setting aside the immense extent of surface over which they are spread, their configuration and features are totally different, and probably their origin also.
>
> Some hold that the whole of the vast region over which they extend was once submerged, and there is much to be said in support of this theory. They appear, however, under various forms, and from observation I should divide them into three great divisions: the 'oak-openings;'—the rich level or rolling Prairie interspersed with belts and points of timber;—and the vast sterile Prairies of the Far West.
>
> And first the 'oak-openings;' so termed from their distinctive feature of the varieties of oak which are seen scattered over them, interspersed at times with pine, black walnut, and other forest trees, which spring from a rich

vegetable soil, generally adapted to the purposes of agriculture. The land is ordinarily dry and rolling. The trees are of medium growth, and rise from a grassy turf seldom encumbered with brushwood, but not unfrequently broken by jungles of rich and gaudy flowering plants, and of dwarf sumac. Among the 'oak-openings' you find some of the most lovely landscapes of the West, and travel for miles and miles through varied park scenery of natural growth, with all the diversity of gently swelling hill and dale—here, trees grouped, or standing single—and there, arranged in long avenues as though by human hands, with slips of open meadow between. Sometimes the openings are interspersed with numerous clear lakes, and with this addition become enchantingly beautiful. But few of these reservoirs have any apparent inlet and outlet. They are fed by subterraneous springs or the rains, and lose their surplus waters by evaporation. Many lie in singularly formed hollows, reflecting in their clear bosoms the varied scenery of the swelling banks, and the alternation of wood and meadow. Michigan and Illinois abound with these 'oak-openings.' Beyond the Mississippi they also occur; but there they hardly form a distinct feature, while on this side they would appear to form a transition from the dense American forest to the wider 'rolling prairie,' which further west ordinarily bounds the thick forest without any such character of country intervening.*

The western Great Lakes area did not begin to share in the westward movement until after 1820. At the time of its creation in 1805, the entire Michigan territory contained a mere handful of people in the area later comprising both Michigan and Wisconsin. In spite of the age of the posts which were founded by the French, Americans had almost no information about the interior. Even after the close of the war of 1812, southern Michigan was assumed to be a swampland.

---

* Charles Joseph Latrobe, *The Rambler in North America* (London, 1835). II, 218-19.

Several factors combined to attract settlers in large numbers in the twenties and thirties. It was definitely demonstrated that the land was well adapted to the needs of farmers. Indian titles to lands were rapidly terminated by the understanding and able administrator, Lewis Cass, who served as territorial governor. Steamboats on the Great Lakes made possible a faster and less expensive journey from the East. This development, coupled with the completion of the Erie Canal, resulted in a large-scale movement in which New England and western New York furnished the majority of settlers. The rapid construction of roads into the interior hastened the growth. In 1834, Michigan had passed the 60,000 population figure, the prerequisite for statehood. Although a state government became operative in 1835, a boundary dispute with Ohio delayed the formal admission until 1837.

Settlement was very slow in Wisconsin until after the defeat, in 1832, of Black Hawk, a leader of the Sioux and Fox Indians. After the cession of land by the defeated Indians, homeseekers did not confine themselves to earlier settled Lake Michigan and Mississippi areas. Thousands took over the rich farm lands of the interior. Although Wisconsin did not become a state until 1848, at that date its population was over 200,000.

The remaining states of the Middle West, with the exception of a small portion of Minnesota, were carved out of the Louisiana Purchase. By this famous purchase, made in 1803, the United States acquired more than 900,000 square miles. At the time, Americans knew little about this vast area acquired from France.

One of the most famous explorations, Captain Meriwether Lewis' and Lieutenant William Clark's, reached the Pacific in 1805, and their report gave only slight—but exciting—information about the great new West. Equally stimulating were the reports of Lieutenant Zebulon Pike—his name is immortalized in Pike's Peak—who set out to explore the headwaters of the Mississippi. Many settlers, however, soon migrated to present-day Louisiana, Missouri and Arkansas. Beginning in the thirties others were drawn to the prairie lands farther north. The defeat of Black Hawk was followed by a rush of settlers to Iowa. Both the native American settlers and the European immigrants sought the now-prized prairie lands of Iowa. A territorial government was organized in 1838, with statehood following in 1846.

Although large-scale settlement did not begin in Minnesota until 1850, both native-born Americans and European immigrants were attracted by the good soil. When Minnesota became a state in 1857, both St. Paul, the capital, and Minneapolis were commercial cities of real significance.

The early history of Kansas was marked by controversy. The Kansas-Nebraska Act of 1854 repealed the Missouri Compromise and opened vast areas of rich western country to slavery. Congressional leaders assumed that at the time of statehood Kansas would be slave and Nebraska free. Anti-slavery people, however, were determined to prevent the admission of Kansas as a slave state. "Bleeding Kansas" was the scene of pitched battles in which both slave and free settlers jockeyed for control. After six bloody years the anti-slavery forces won. On January 29, 1861, Kansas, with a free constitution, was admitted as the thirty-fourth state.

By 1860 the Middle West had captured the imagination of millions. The growth of the Old Northwest, in particular, was truly phenomenal. In 1860 the combined population of its five states was almost 6,000,000, or 17 per cent of the population of the entire nation. New York and Pennsylvania were the first and second largest states, respectively, in population; but Ohio was third with 2,239,000 inhabitants. The population of Illinois was 1,711,000; Indiana

1,350,000; Wisconsin 775,000; and Michigan 749,000. The other states did not lag. Iowa had a population of 674,000. The recently created state of Minnesota had 172,000 inhabitants. Kansas, still a territory, had a population of 170,000.

The basic character of this expanding Middle West was determined by the pioneers who wanted to make a new society in something of the pattern they already knew and respected. Although no pioneer is a stereotype, observers commented that a persisting characteristic of the westward movement was the hope of those who made the journey—following a lengthy journey in which, too often, some element of danger was always present—to their new homes with an unrestrained and unusual optimistic confidence in the future. Another circumstance, strange to those who did not understand the ways of the American pioneer, was the comparative ease with which men and women adjusted to their new situations. A large number were seemingly "at home" even in the wilderness settlements. Obviously, a large number of Americans, who were vitally influenced by their pioneering experiences, retained the memories of their common experiences.

New settlers in the West included both the native-born, contributed from all of the other states, and the European immigrants who became increasingly numerous after the middle thirties. The great majority of prospective farmers had some knowledge of husbandry. Many who came to the West arrived without adequate (or practically no) capital. Others, among the homeseekers, had ample means to withstand even several consecutive lean years.

Frequently settlers migrated to the Middle West within a communal framework. It was not unusual for families to band together to assure the taking over of a large portion of a township. This process was also employed in some instances by the recently arrived Europeans.

Adjustments to the new environment were many. Some information about the new country was available before the first permanent farm settlers moved into the country in which both the hunters and fur traders had served as pathfinders. The latter, because of their daring, were of major importance in paving the way for the prospective farmers. A final step, normally, in community development was attained with the arrival of men with sufficient capital to engage in advanced agriculture or business enterprises.

The first year in the new area was always critical for a settler. In these very few months he had to build a cabin, plant a crop, and, in spare moments, build his furniture. If a pioneer could clear even three acres during the first year, he considered the season a success. Farmers with but little capital always found it necessary also to improve much of their own farm equipment. During the first year after the acquisition of land, many pioneers were practically isolated and unable to shop in a town of any size.

The first major task of the settler was to erect some kind of shelter, however temporary. In many wooded areas, a log cabin, about 18 feet by 22 feet, was almost standard. This first cabin was often constructed without nails, and might remain floorless for several years. The settler would install glass windows only after his farm began to pay and when he could purchase supplies from a nearby town. In many communities glass was a surprisingly scarce item. The settler made the household furniture, whenever possible, from the materials on his own farm. The famous community bee, an established institution in the Middle West, provided free labor to erect the larger farm buildings.

Except in the prairie areas the settler frequently met his food requirements by hunting and fishing. The pioneer was very much of a woodsman. Few dared to challenge the frontier without their own firearms. The diet of the pioneer family would never satisfy the standard of our contemporary dieticians, although protein demands were more than met with a menu rich in venison, bear meat, wild turkey and wild geese, and pork. Practically every farmer cured his own pork. At first, flour was scarce and the farm diet had little starch. Many farmers resorted to pumpkin bread. Vegetables could always be grown, but many farmers could not afford the time to work a garden. In many areas, wild berries regularly supplemented the diet. Until canning became practical, few vegetables could be raised for more than immediate consumption. During the first portion of the pioneer era, the average family actually could not afford to purchase coffee or tea, and resorted to beverages made from home-grown herbs. These drinks had apparently quite unpredictable tastes and were almost invariably known as green tea. Most families had their own facilities for storing wheat, flour, corn meal, salt pork, and potatoes. In many areas, the settlers depended upon maple syrup or honey for sweetening. Maple syrup was not always immediately consumed or made into sugar, since many housewives partially boiled the syrup to produce a liquid which was in turn allowed to ferment and then used as a specialized vinegar.

The settler's wife usually had a minimum of cooking utensils. A single frying pan and a few kettles might tide over the average settler's family for several years. The settler's wife did all baking and cooking in a crude fireplace. Even household cleanliness was harder to attain than we might now assume, since the brooms had to be home-constructed.

The agrarian pioneers were aided by the liberal land policies of the government. A provision of 1785 had provided for the sale of 640 acres at one dollar an acre. However, the number of direct purchases of 640-acre tracts from the government was smaller than had been anticipated. Consequently, in 1796, though the minimum price of land was increased to two dollars an acre, the law made provisions for credit for one year. However, these new terms still did not satisfy the average prospective purchaser, who insisted that both the minimum price and minimum acreage sold were beyond his means.

In 1800 the procedure accordingly was changed to provide for the sale of 320 acres, soon amended to 160, at $2.00 per acre. A pioneer could obtain such a block of land on a credit basis of one-fourth down with the balance to be paid in three annual payments. The establishment of land offices at convenient locations also stimulated sales. During the next two decades the government actually sold over 18,000,000 acres of land. In this twenty-year period, the peak sales, approximately 3,500,000 acres, were reported in 1818.

In 1820 the panic, which began in 1819, was felt universally. The governmental land policy became a subject of heated political discussion. Many purchasers insisted that the credit provisions should be liberalized. Others maintained that the credit features were unsatisfactory because many of the purchases, especially by speculators, reverted to the government. Under this further pressure, in 1820 Congress reduced the price of land to $1.25 an acre and abandoned the credit provisions. The minimum acreage sold was lowered to 80 acres and later reduced to 40 acres. These new policies reflect a responsiveness by the government to the needs of future farmers instead of the former primary objective of securing revenue.

Although millions of acres of land were available at these low prices, many ambitious farmers still lacked the necessary cash to make the required payments. The new policies of the government did not entirely bar squatter settlers, though they had no legal claim to land. Many ambitious men settled on the land in advance of surveys and settlements. Under a system known as pre-emption, after they had accumulated the purchase price, these men were given the right of buying the land which they had already improved. Although the Congress originally hoped to discourage this practice, Congress also determined to play generously with the westerners who were without land titles. In 1801 Congress passed the first effective legislation to aid the squatter. By 1841, it had legally recognized pre-emption as a fixed principle in the process of land distribution.

The acquisition of a farm by the process of pre-emption required a degree of real individual daring. In an age when a large portion of the population lived from farming—and rather successfully so—it was generally assumed that any barrier to land ownership was thus the equivalent of a denial of opportunity. Consequently, pressure groups urged legislation that would enable each well-qualified prospective farmer to receive a free tract or homestead from the government. This pressure was further increased as the number of unskilled workers in the cities increased. Reformers began to visualize land ownership as an escape from poverty.

The case for a liberal land policy was strengthened by the argument that large tracts had been assigned to the states for special purchases. Some of these grants had been made specifically for education while other assignments were earmarked for internal improvements. Likewise, Congress had granted to the states millions of acres which were described as swamplands to be reclaimed by drainage.

This general idea of land reform was widely and enthusiastically promoted by a surprising number of our best early publicists. Perhaps the best known champion was Henry Evans who organized associations and lectured tirelessly and everywhere. Horace Greeley, the famous editor of the New York *Tribune,* was among Evans's supporters. Greeley's own editorials won many converts to the cause of free land.

By 1848, these homestead champions were a powerful wing in the Free Soil Party whose nominee for the presidency was ex-president Martin Van Buren. The Party also was antislavery and the champion of various other reforms. Its platform declared: "that the free grant to actual settlers, in consideration of the expenses they incur in making settlements in the wilderness, which are usually fully equal to their actual cost, and of the public benefits resulting there from, of reasonable portions of the public lands, under suitable limitations, is a wise and just measure of public policy which will promote, in various ways, the interests of all the states of this Union; and we therefore recommend it to the favorable consideration of the American people." Many leaders of each of the major parties also advocated homesteads. Several states passed laws which made their swamplands available to homesteaders.

In the administration of President Buchanan, Congress approved a compromise measure to reduce the price of land to 25 cents an acre, but Buchanan vetoed this measure. In 1850, the Republicans championed the homestead reform and this strengthened their new party among farmers who wanted to make certain that their children and grandchildren would, in their turn, be assured of economic opportunities.

Victory came to the champions of free lands on May 20, 1862, with the approval of the Morrill Act which granted 160 acres of land free. This act required only that the individual live on his farm for five years before he could acquire title. The measure was partially nullified by the fact that much of the land was located in areas where 160 acres could not adequately support a family. Of course, many could not raise enough money to make the trip and to buy essential equipment. Nevertheless, the Morrill Act brought economic independence to thousands.

The absence of adequate transportation facilities was a

major, and sometimes almost insurmountable, barrier in the economic progress of many portions of the Middle West. The majority of the settlers came to understand that an improvement in transportation facilities would bring closer social ties, as well as the many economic advantages resulting from the promotion of commerce. During the first half of the nineteenth century, in particular, much attention was given to the development of an adequate transportation system. Because of this emphasis roads were improved, canals constructed, thousands of miles of railways were built, and the steamboat became a fixture on the Great Lakes and the leading river systems.

Before the invention of the steam vessel, American ingenuity had developed many craft for the western rivers. These river boats, constructed to meet the immediate needs, served as magnificent media of transportation beginning in the late eighteenth century. Although uniformity in construction was not emphasized, we can distinguish several patterns. The pirogue was made of logs and was most frequently forty feet in length. It could carry a cargo of several tons. It was propelled downstream by oars and upstream by poles. The bateau was a larger and more refined version of the pirogue. Out of it, Ohio people developed the keelboat. Its equipment included a mast and sail, and it was accordingly able to take advantage of the wind. Because of its greater size, it ordinarily carried a crew, whose chief physical labor was to get the boat upstream. Skilled polemen among a crew numbering from ten to twenty were men of understandable prestige in the river country.

Another standard design was the ark. It was designed solely for downriver trips and was dismantled at the end of the journey. The chief advantage of the ark was its inexpensive construction. Some were built solely to transport a single family and its goods; others were of considerable length and could carry a large cargo. The slow barges were serviceable for heavy freight and carried a crew equal to that of the keelboat. Barges were effective in both down- and upstream traffic. The flatboat was also common. It was cheaply constructed, primarily for the purpose of carrying freight. At the downstream destination, the flatboat was usually sold outright for timber. The pride of the great Ohio River was the packet. It combined features of the barge and keelboat and carried both passengers and freight. Some captains included a number of conveniences, such as cabins and stoves, in an effort to compete with barges. All of the river craft were slow. The trip upstream from New Orleans to Pittsburgh frequently required four months. The slowness of this service of course increased the costs of shipment upstream.

The steam vessel gradually replaced the slow river craft. The first of these steam vessels was *The New Orleans*. It was built in Pittsburgh at a cost of $38,000. It left Pittsburgh on October 20, 1811, and with frequent and long stops, reached New Orleans on January 10, 1812, and thus proved that the new means of transportation could operate advantageously on the Mississippi system.

Within a few years, as the result of frequent changes in design, a distinct and inexpensive type of river steam vessel was developed. All except the fastest passenger steamers made numerous stops to load and unload local freight. Even the speedier boats made numerous stops for fueling, and the passengers themselves frequently helped to load the wood.

At first, steamboats were extensively used only on the lower Ohio and Mississippi. In 1832, a vessel went northward to the Falls of St. Anthony, site of the Twin Cities, in Minnesota. Others ventured up the Missouri. Regular service was established to Fort Leavenworth [Kansas], in 1829 and Fort Pierce [South Dakota], in 1831. By the outbreak of the Civil War, the entire Mississippi and nearly all of its tributaries were part of a gigantic steamboat system. Inasmuch as a large portion of this vast territory was not adequately served by canals and railroads before the Civil War, the owners of steam vessels received rich returns upon their investments. Records indicate that some boats returned a profit of double the cost of construction in a single year.

Steamboats had a definite superiority over the barges, keel boats, and flat boats in carrying passengers because of the rapid service and near-luxurious facilities. They also carried much freight upstream—frequently at rates considerably lower than those of the other kinds of boats—and slowly they displaced these other boats.

The new means of transportation greatly speeded the expansion of commerce. It was one of the basic factors influencing the development of the Mississippi Valley trade. As early as 1840, New Orleans was a major world port. Although this great north-south flow of internal commerce on the Ohio and Mississippi rivers was challenged by later transportation developments, it remained important long after the Civil War. Cincinnati and other river cities shared in the gains of New Orleans.

As early as 1816, a steam vessel operated on Lake Ontario. The possibilities of the steamboat, however, were more successfully demonstrated by the *Walk-in-the-Water,* which made the run from Buffalo to Detroit in forty-four hours in 1818. This pioneer vessel was assembled at Black Rock, later incorporated within Buffalo, with an engine made in New York. Since this was before the completion of the Erie Canal, a month was required to transport the machinery from Albany to Buffalo by wagon. The *Walk-in-the-Water,* whose schedule of fare was eighteen dollars for cabin passengers and nine dollars for the steerage, was the forerunner of numerous vessels that drastically reduced the schedules for travel between the East and the Great Lakes ports of the Middle West. Businessmen in leading Lake Erie cities invested heavily in steamship construction and operation. By the middle thirties, thousands of emigrants from the East annually reached new homes in the growing West by traveling on the Erie Canal packet boats to Buffalo where they took lake boats for Detroit and other western cities.

By 1860, the steamships on the Lakes, including Lake Superior, numbered over 350 and had a total tonnage almost half of that of the sailing vessels. The lake steam vessels often matched ocean steamers in elegance and comfort, and though they carried some light freight, they were primarily passenger boats. Until after the Civil War, when steam freighters became more common, sailing vessels were used to transport most of the bulky freight, since low shipment costs were the primary consideration. When through-railroad lines were completed in the fifties, the majority of western homeseekers used them instead of the slower boat service. As a result, Chicago rapidly displaced Detroit as the center for immigrants moving to the West.

Many eastern areas constructed turnpikes. The turnpike, a type of road which originated in England, derived its name from the long poles, with pikes placed across the road at the points where the tolls were collected. The term turnpike, however, was commonly employed to indicate any type of improved highway.

The most important single turnpike to serve the Middle West was the Cumberland or National Road, whose construction was undertaken by the federal government. As early as 1802 Congress approved of a plan whereby a portion of the receipts from the sale of public lands within Ohio could be used to build a road to unite the new state and the East. Pressure from the West resulted in approval in 1806 for a highway to extend from the Atlantic Coast to the

Mississippi River. The eastern terminal was Cumberland, Maryland, which was already connected with Baltimore, a major turnpike terminal, by the Frederick Turnpike. The contracts for the first stages of construction were authorized in 1811. Seven years later the highway was completed to the Ohio River. It was extended westward to Columbus, Ohio, by 1833. Although some sums for surveys and extensions were later voted, Congressional appropriations for construction practically ended in 1838. The total cost to the government by the time that it reached Vandalia, Illinois, in 1852, was $7,000,000. Although the highway was projected as a free road, Congress relinquished its control to the states and they charged tolls.

The National Road was planned as a road eighty feet in width. A wide central section was covered with stone and gravel. These construction plans were carried out only so far as Indiana. Enthusiasm for the road was not great in the forties and fifties, when one's imagination was stirred by visions of canals and railroads. As a result, the extreme western portion of the highway differed little from many of the other dirt roads.

The highway called attention to the value of the lengthy artery of transportation. Immigrants to the West made use of this through route. It also carried through freight in a volume that pointed to the railroads of the future. Zanesville, Columbus, and Springfield in Ohio, and Richmond, Indianapolis, and Terre Haute in Indiana are among the cities whose development was furthered by the highway.

The most radical changes in transportation, however, resulted from the construction of canals and railroads. Between 1815 and 1830, Americans seem to have favored the canals. During the early thirties, their interest was divided almost between the two. By the forties, Americans were clearly less enthusiastic about the canals.

Both private corporations and state governments undertook the construction of canals and railroads. In their initial ventures, the midwestern states were forced to rely almost exclusively upon their public treasuries, supplemented by some land grants. The panic of 1837 of course retarded all economic development and reduced the sizes of the public programs of canal construction and the pace of railroad building.

The completion of the Erie Canal in 1825 marked the beginning of a new era in transportation. The potentialities of the canal were recognized by others than New Yorkers. Ambitious proposals were immediately advanced in other states.

Political expediency was often a factor in determining the number of projects and routes in the midwestern states where the programs called for a detailed legislative approval of the huge public expenditures. In Ohio, Indiana, and Illinois, the general plans usually outlined the building of canals with terminals at ports on the Great Lakes. These states thus became less dependent upon the Mississippi and instead united this growing and wealthy region with the East. These canals carried a substantial amount of freight and enjoyed an important role in the transportation network until the network of railroads was in effective operation after the middle of the century.

Ohio inaugurated its canal program in 1825. On July 4, Governor Clinton of New York most appropriately dug the first spadeful of earth, and Governor Morrow of Ohio was the second at the projected Ohio Canal, designed to link Portsmouth and Cleveland. Workmen also immediately began the construction of the Miami and Erie to unite Cincinnati and Toledo. The Ohio Canal was completed by 1833. The Miami and Erie was extended northward to Dayton by 1834, and with federal aid was later continued to

Toledo. These two major canals, together with branch lines, gave the state a really impressive network.

A canal charter was issued in Indiana as early as 1805. Although the stock was tax exempt, subscriptions did not produce sufficient capital to warrant construction. The canal era brought a different response. In part because of federal aid, the state over-enthusiastically outlined an unusually ambitious program of canals, which was begun just before the crash of 1837. The only important canal completed was the Wabash and Erie. This connected Lafayette and Toledo, Ohio, with the sanction of Ohio, in 1843. It was extended to Evansville in 1854, but at that date the feverish interest in canals was subsiding.

Despite an earlier authorization and some federal aid, Illinois did not launch her program until 1836. Following the example of Ohio, construction of the Illinois and Michigan Canal began on July 4. This canal was planned to connect the Mississippi and the Great Lakes by the improvement of the Illinois River westward from Chicago, and was finally completed in 1848. Work on other projects was halted by the financial crash of 1837.

Michigan had shown an interest in canals during the territorial period. Statehood, officially attained in 1837, enabled Michigan to embark upon an ambitious program of internal improvements which included plans for a network of small canals. Although some initial construction was undertaken on one artery, the panic retarded the building of state-owned canals. In the 1830's the Michigan legislature rejected the proposal to build the St. Mary's Falls ship canal to link Lakes Superior and Michigan. The discovery of copper and iron deposits in the Upper Peninsula of Michigan revived interest in the project. In 1852, Congress granted the state land to finance the construction of the canal whose locks at the time were the largest in the world.

The canal ultimately became a major gateway to the West and was transferred to the federal government in 1881.

The canals fostered internal commerce by providing a medium for the transportation of bulk cargoes. In many midwestern areas, before the construction of canals, freight rates were 70 cents per ton mile. Rates on the Ohio Canal in 1853 were one cent. Some canal rates averaged as low as .25 cents.

Then, in turn, the canal was displaced. Climatic conditions limited operations only to a few months each year. The time-consuming repairs caused frequent and lengthy delays. The canals ultimately were unable to meet the competition of the greater speed and flexibility of the railroads.

The railroad was financed by a combination of private enterprise, state governments, and federal aid and became the next medium for solving the transportation problem. Obviously, highways were not the answer to the transportation difficulties. At best only a portion of the great Middle West could be served by natural waterways. Canal construction called for huge expenditures and was completely impractical in many regions. Although its waterway rivals continued to carry huge cargoes, the railroad had the great advantage of adaptability. It could be built in any part of the country. Sidings literally reached the doors of many business establishments. It could speedily transport goods and passengers from any point and could guarantee service in any season. No other form of transportation at the time would have made possible the rapid settlement of the Middle West.

The first railroad to establish service in the Middle West was the Erie and Kalamazoo. In 1836 it began regular transportation between Toledo, Ohio and Adrian, Michigan Territory. It lacked adequate capital and was driven into bankruptcy in the following year. Its failure, however, did not discourage further railroad construction in the Middle West.

Although competition, including owners of stage coach lines, and alarmists, who feared either monopolies or the consequences of any innovation, stood ready to oppose, two forms of financing the railroads assured their success during the period of initial development. First, private capital was sufficient for the numerous small lines that were built in areas already well populated. Profits were almost assured in advance. Secondly, the railroad was soon included in many of the state internal improvement programs where it seemed to offer a practical solution when canal construction was questionable.

State governments adopted liberal policies in order to encourage railways. Usually charters granted the privilege of eminent domain. In many instances no restrictions were imposed upon the methods of financing. Some lines were exempted in part, or even in entirety, from taxation.

Since any spectacular development lends itself to promotional schemes some abuses resulted from railroad financing. Stockholders, who furnished but little capital, often directed policies of railways built with capital furnished by the bondholders. This practice, which was more common in the infancy of the industry, aided professional promoters.

Although some towns contributed to the construction of railroads, their aid was insignificant in comparison with the formal encouragement given by states. Some of the states confined their assistance to loans, while others made free surveys and land grants. Ohio authorized liberal stock subscriptions. Irregular promotional practices in Ohio resulted from a state agreement to purchase one-third of the stock in any company when the initial two-thirds had been subscribed.

Several of the states undertook a program of public ownership. The most ambitious projects were outlined in the rapidly growing midwestern states. Only minor portions of the proposed networks, however, were completed by the states which could not finance internal improvements in a depression. Several of the states defaulted in payment of the huge debts incurred from internal improvements. In a few instances the arrears represented a partial repudiation of the debts. Illinois was forced to abandon plans calling for 1,300 miles of state constructed railways. Michigan sold her two public operated lines to private investors in 1846.

After public ownership was abandoned, many turned to the federal government for assistance in constructing railroads in undeveloped areas where private capital was not available. Congress was already committed to a policy of encouragement of internal improvements. A measure of 1824 provided the services of engineers for the planning and development of railways.

Although the Baltimore and Ohio hoped to receive aid from the federal government through stock subscription, this proposal was rejected. Various attempts from a number of companies to secure subscriptions or loans also failed. Some members of Congress were apparently willing to help railroads if in return the carriers agreed to transport mail free of further charges.

However, Congress frequently did grant public lands to railroads for a right of way. Petitions for such grants became increasingly numerous. In 1850, Illinois was given almost 2,600,000 acres of public lands which the state in turn granted to the Illinois Central. In 1852, Congress authorized for an interval of ten years extensive right of way privileges through the public domain. Later on, this generous policy was further liberalized.

As a result of adequate financing, the program of railroad construction moved forward rapidly. By 1853 an all-rail route operated between the major cities of the East and Chicago. In the following year a railroad was completed from Chicago to Rock Island, Illinois, on the Mississippi River. In 1859 train service was established between Chicago and the Gulf of Mexico. By 1860 Chicago, with eleven railroads, had established its reputation as the major railway city of the nation.

In 1860 the nation had 30,000 miles of railroads. Ohio led with approximately 3,000 miles. The Illinois figure, 2,800, was almost identical with the national mileage in 1840. Even remote Iowa could boast of 655 miles of track.

The expansion of the railway network and the lowering of tariffs ultimately enabled the railroad to capture a larger share of the freight traffic. The railways, of course, gained an easy advantage as carriers of bulk in areas not served by competitive forms of transportation. As early as the forties, coal was an important source of income to some companies. The less bulky freight was shipped by rail even where water routes were rivals. This is well illustrated by the Chicago market. Chicago sent its grain to eastern terminals by water but used the railways for the shipment of many of its other products. Largely as a result of the railroads, although canals made their contributions, commerce followed east-west lines instead of north-south.

The Civil War is a dividing point in American history. Union victory in the struggle was the result of many circumstances. Military historians have, with details, recorded the strategy and campaigns of successful generals. In the last analysis, however, the North won because of a superiority in manpower and economic resources. The economy of the Union was able to absorb strains while the structure of the Confederacy collapsed.

Throughout the entire Civil War the contributions made

by the Middle West to the Union cause were impressive. Each state furnished a significant number of men to the armed services. Many of the regiments registered a frightening number of casualties. In every community the various home front activities supplemented the contributions in men.

Industrial productivity in the Middle West attained new levels. The most notable gains were made in the cities with good transportation facilities. The agricultural output was increased by the use of machinery. The recently developed railroad network assured the transportation of men, food, and the essential manufactured products.

After the Civil War the frontier remained a magic term. Land was taken up at a faster rate even than before 1860. Rapid settlement brought statehood to Nebraska (1867), North Dakota (1889), and South Dakota (1889).

Settlers speedily converted vast areas of wilderness into productive farms. Literally hundreds of new communities in the Middle West were created in the pattern of the agrarian settlements of the pre-Civil War era. The unusual growth in the trans-Mississippi area was matched by similar gains in the older states of the Middle West where prospective farmers purchased the remaining suitable farm land, including even the timber cutover acreage. Between 1870 and 1900 the population of the Dakotas increased from 14,000 to 720,000. The population increase in many rural counties of Michigan and Wisconsin was in the proportion of the growth in the Dakotas.

The future Indian policy posed a major question to all frontier people. For years, the Indian was among the foremost of the barriers to western expansion. Experience had shown that many of the tribes in the West were not hostile to the Americans. On the other hand, the Sioux, northern Cheyenne, and Arapaho, the most important of the tribes of the northern plains, were determined to preserve their own way of life at all costs. These groups were largely dependent upon the buffalo, and the men were remarkable horsemen and marksmen—qualities that also produced good warriors.

During the Civil War, the Indians, who were accustomed to freedom of action over a vast region, engaged in numerous raids against the frontier settlements. Their expeditions included attacks upon both the stage coaches and traders. These actions demanded large-scale military action. Because of the pressing demands of Union generals in this very critical year of the Civil War, in November 1864, a Colorado volunteer force was formed, and under the leadership of Colonel J. M. Chivington, killed over 500 Indians in retaliation.

Indian campaigns then ceased temporarily. In 1865, they were resumed, however, on a large scale, to begin more than ten years of warfare requiring the use of Federal troops. Many of the outstanding military men of the nation were engaged in the defense of western settlements. The extermination of the buffalo and the continuous military pressure resulted in ultimate defeat for the tribes of the Northern Plains. Yet the toll was often heavy, and among the many casualties of Indian warfare was the famous George A. Custer who, in his twenties, rose to the rank of major general in the Civil War.

Most Americans sincerely hoped that our government could devise an Indian policy to end this bloodshed. As early as the fifties, many Pacific Coast Indians had been established on reservations, where they were given supplies and other assistance. In 1871, Congress virtually imposed the reservation system upon all except a small minority of the Indian population. By the late seventies, hundreds of Indian children were attending government reservation schools. Reservation life, however, had numerous disadvantages. The new mode of life was resented by the older generation. A large number of Indians resented their new status as wards and asserted, plausibly enough, that it labeled their people as inferior. Many American students of Indian affairs also attacked the new policy.

In 1887, Congress passed the Dawes Act. This was an attempt to integrate the Indian nations within the American political, economic, and social life. This measure dissolved the tribes as legal units and instead gave each Indian specific farm allotments from the tribal lands previously set aside by the government. At the end of a twenty-five year interval, Indians were to be admitted to full citizenship and were to be free to sell their lands. Although this policy was frequently modified, Indian resistance to Western settlement was, for all practical purposes, ended.

Prospective farmers undoubtedly went to the newer regions of the Middle West with greater hopes for the future than had earlier generations. Adequate railroad facilities not only assured markets but also tended to remove the isolation of an earlier time. The many technological advances eased the burden both of farming and homemaking.

Yet discomforts, and frequently hardships, of life were inevitable in any new environment. No farmer could survive without water. The developments in well-digging and the utilization of especially designed metal windmills helped to solve the problem of water in prairie areas. Technology likewise contributed to settlement on the plains with the invention of the barbed wire used in fence construction. Although rival claimants were numerous, Joseph F. Glidden, who secured a patent in 1874, is ordinarily regarded as the originator of the idea. The barbed wire fence gave the individual farmer a protection against the roving cattlemen. Although fencing was a prime enemy of cattlemen, the new practice made possible the more rapid establishment of farms in the West.

Homeseekers were reminded of the potentialities of the West by the railroads which directed their appeals to the native born and the immigrant. The promotional bulletins published by the railroads are among our most valuable sources of contemporary conditions; for they give details similar to those published by gazetteers earlier in the century. Naturally, it was to the advantage of a railroad to attract a population that would utilize its service. Companies, also, were anxious to sell the acreage that had been received in the form of land grants.

Government policies of land distribution played an unusually significant role in the rapid development of new areas. Although the Homestead Act provided, with qualifications, for free land, other measures were also of great importance in determining the trends and patterns of settlement. The reclamation and irrigation programs made possible the utilization of thousands of acres of land for profitable agriculture. The granting of large portions of the public domain to the states and railroads likewise hastened the westward movement. An immigration policy, virtually without restriction, added to the number of newcomers. Although many immigrants settled in the East, large numbers eagerly sought homes in the new communities.

In portions of the Middle West lumbering was the stimulus for settlement. At the middle of the nineteenth century, New York, Pennsylvania, and Maine were the leading states in the industry, which could boast of a production of five billion feet of lumber. By 1880, however, the white pine of the Great Lakes had created the great lumbering industries in Michigan, Wisconsin, and Minnesota. These states sold lumber both to the eastern markets and to the expanding Chicago market which served as a source of supply for the prairie states.

In 1870 Michigan ranked first in the nation in the production of board feet. Next to agriculture, the industry had become the most important in the state. A gradual decline, however, began after 1890. Nevertheless, as late as 1935, some 4,000 men were employed in lumbering activities. The virgin standing pine in Wisconsin has been estimated at 129 billion feet. Yet, much of this had been cut and marketed by 1890. With some few exceptions the great timber resources of Wisconsin had been depleted by 1919. The peak of Minnesota lumbering was reached late in the nineteenth century.

The two fundamental processes in lumbering were logging and milling. Logging included all steps from the selection of the trees to be cut to their conversion into logs. In milling the logs were processed into a variety of products including board lumber, shingles, and railroad ties.

The impact of logging in particular is obvious in many areas, even today. Despite the fact that many denuded areas later became sites of a thriving agricultural life, far too many of these depleted regions must be called simply "cutover." Often they are characterized by a precarious part-time farming and a general absence of trading centers of any great wealth. Fortunately, in recent years the tourist trade has revived the economy of many "cutover" areas.

Thriving centers emerged as small cities at the mouths of the river systems utilized for transporting the logs. Saginaw, Muskegon, Traverse City, and Green Bay are but a few of the many cities that owe their early development to their importance as mill towns. After 1890 lumber mills were often built in cities already well established. This is understandable; since the industry, with the construction of railroads, had become less dependent upon the railroads. The important mill towns were stable communities whose operations were carried on throughout the entire year.

The most successful lumbering entrepreneurs engaged both in logging and milling. The leaders in the industry have often been severely criticized for the waste that resulted from their hearty attempts to denude the forests. Many owners, however, apparently did not realize that the forest reserves would be so rapidly exhausted. Likewise, it was almost essential for them to utilize their resources hurriedly since they always faced losses from market fluctuations and the potential danger of forest fires.

The lumbering industry accelerated the growth of transportation facilities, especially by encouraging the construction of railroads which were afforded revenue through the carrying of timber products. The related industries, especially production of furniture, paper, agricultural implements, carriages and wagons, and even some of the chemical fields received a stimulus from lumbering.

The search for minerals brought many to the Middle West. In the middle eighteen seventies, thousands joined in a mad rush to the Black Hills of South Dakota following the announcement of the discovery of gold. But here they promptly encountered such technological obstacles that few mining towns developed. Disappointed, they learned that Dakota gold could be extracted and processed only with equipment requiring vast outlays of capital.

In a sense, the pattern for the permanent mining community was established in the Great Lakes area. Early in the eighteen forties, Dr. Douglas Houghton, the state geologist of Michigan, in his masterful reports, mentioned the presence of rich copper deposits in the western portion of the Upper Peninsula. By the middle of the decade, a large-scale copper fever had developed. Even prior to the Civil

War, many corporations, financed with eastern capital, were formed to tap the copper resources. Michigan's reputation as the greatest copper producing state, however, was established by the Calumet and Hecla Company This corporation represented in part an amalgamation of smaller concerns and operated the most productive copper mine in the nation. The capital of $10,000,000 was the basis of a structure which paid over $160,000,000 to the shareholders.

Pioneer iron mining operations in the Lake Superior region began in 1847. The first mines, with their limited capital, were unprofitable because of high transportation costs, the universal expenses of operation in a region where necessary commodities were imported at a high cost, and finally, because the industry was not adapted to the principle of smelting in this area.

The transportation problem was partially solved with the completion, in 1855, of the Sault Canal. Likewise, feasible techniques of mining were introduced. Companies gradually abandoned the practice of smelting and instead transported the raw ore to the new specialized market in the East. It was also found that iron mining could be undertaken successfully only by the employment of large-scale methods. Consolidation similar to those in the copper industry took place. The new companies with the larger capital constructed improved transportation facilities and equipped themselves with the latest technological discoveries. By 1900 the Lake Superior iron region, consisting of northern Michigan and Wisconsin and northeastern Minnesota, furnished seventy-six per cent of the iron ore mined in the central states. Vessels of enormous capacity transferred the ore from docks at Marquette, Ashland, Duluth, and other Lake Superior ports to the Lake Erie ports, where powerful cranes unloaded them with breathtaking rapidity, and also to the mills in the Chicago area.

Although the railroads became an accepted fixture in the Midwestern scene long before the Civil War, the period of their dramatically rapid construction did not really come until after the close of that gigantic struggle. The panic of 1873, of course, retarded many construction projects. Yet, in spite of these financial ills, more miles were added. Throughout the decade of the eighties, the railroads undertook unprecedented construction.

In 1870, Iowa had 2,600 miles in operation. In 1900, the figure was 8,700. During the same interval the miles in operation in Kansas increased from 1,500 to 8,700. The mileage in Nebraska increased from 700 to 5,600. In Minnesota the mileage increased from 1,000 to 6,500. In 1870 South Dakota had a meager 65 miles in operation. Three decades later the figure was 2,800. In 1870 North Dakota was without railroads. In 1900 some 2,700 miles were in operation. Gains were significant, also, in the older states. Between 1870 and 1900 the Wisconsin network increased from 1,500 miles to 6,500 miles.

Much of this construction completed the nation's major railroad systems by which Chicago and other Midwestern cities were united even with the once remote Pacific coast. In 1867 Minneapolis and Chicago were linked by rail. On May 1, 1869 hundreds assembled at Promonatory, Utah, to witness the spectacular Golden Spike Ceremony signifying the completion of the first transcontinental line. In 1883 the Middle West and the Pacific Northwest were united by rail. The many great networks of the Middle West reached out to place practically all farmers within fairly easy reach of a station.

The accomplishments and progress in railroading were partially the result of a new attitude. Every conscious effort was made to unite "far flung" markets. Farmers acquired a new confidence when they heard trains lumbering through their communities. Numerous consolidations were effected to weld small lines into major networks. In general, these mergers resulted in both greater efficiency and higher profits.

In this era of expansion, Chicago became the great hub of the railroad networks. Not only did Chicago have connections with the South, but it was also the meeting point of practically all transcontinental companies, and accordingly became the gateway to both the Southwest and the Northwest. Minneapolis and Cincinnati are major railroad centers, but they have always ranked far under Chicago. All of these leading railroad terminal cities promptly became great commercial centers and distribution points.

The railroad, however, rendered its greatest and most dramatic service in previously undeveloped areas. In the early stages of the industry, the railroad followed settlement. In the late nineteenth century the railroad preceded settlement. Contemporaries said that it "made the country." With a few exceptions, the railroad was the only form of transportation that could assure an area a market. Communities reached by the railroad envisioned great future gains, while less fortunate inland towns helplessly saw their growth greatly stunted by a lack of railroad transportation.

The federal government early provided absolutely necessary help in the construction of these railroads by devising a system of land grants. The model for future grants was the Illinois Central grant, made in 1850 with the authorization of a right-of-way of 200 feet through the public domain, supplemented by the alternate sections on both sides of the right-of-way running back for a distance of six miles. The government hoped that the sections, which it retained as a part of the public domain, would increase in value as a result of the railroad. Later grants provided for a wider right-of-way. Also, in some instances, the alternate sections extended back twenty miles on each side of the railway.

Originally, the federal grants were made to the states, which then transferred title to the railways. After 1862, these federal assignments were made directly to the railroad companies.

In return, these land-grant railroads, as they came to be called, agreed to lower rates for the government over the land-grant mileage only. Some companies agreed to transport troops and government property without fees. The definition of many of the involved terms required a great deal of subsequent judicial interpretation. In 1940, Congress modified many of these railroad obligations; and, in 1946, it cancelled the remaining obligations.

These federal grants to the railroads were discontinued after 1871. Many students and critics maintained that this assistance, which was designed to assure transportation in undeveloped areas, was largely abused. The railroads, in turn, have insisted that they have adequately repaid the government for the earlier subsidies.

Both state and local governments encouraged construction by the purchase of railroad stocks. Some communities made outright contributions to railroads. States often contributed to the cost of surveys. To stimulate construction, some states even offered liberal tax exemptions.

The major task of financing, however, was undertaken primarily by private capital. Although many shares were sold to small-scale purchasers, large blocks were frequently purchased by investors of means. Railroad securities were often purchased by foreign investors. In 1899, Europe owned some $3,100,000,000 worth of our railroad securities. The initial construction of the St. Paul and Pacific, forerunner of the Great Northern, was financed by Dutch bankers. James F. Hill was able to acquire control and to enlarge the line only through the assistance of English and Canadian interests.

Some financial ills and downright abuses were part of the cost of this tremendous effort of construction. Too frequently promotion failed to take into consideration essential problems relating to future earning. Technically uninformed boosters of railways sometimes encouraged the building of inefficient narrow gauge lines just because their construction cost was lower than that of the standard gauge. Overcapitalization, better known as stock watering, angered both the investors and the general public. Irregularities of railroad financing were highly publicized and contributed to the demand for regulation.

Cities in the Middle West grew rapidly as the area gradually challenged the industrial supremacy of the East. The industrial climate was favorable for a number of reasons. Inasmuch as modern transportation affords a national market, the concentration of an industry in a particular city or area is ordinarily the result of several factors that assure lower costs of production and distribution. Proximity to sources of supply plays a very significant role. The availability of local capital frequently was the stimulus for successful operations. The extension of credit by local bankers to enterprising individuals was the basis of success on numerous occasions. Costs of initial plant construction, taxation, and availability and charges for power are additional considerations. An outlet for by-products constitutes a factor of importance for some industries. An isolated packing house that lacked a market for hides, tallow, and lard in the same city operated at a disadvantage. Adequate transportation facilities are also determining factors. The labor supply must include a reserve both of skilled and unskilled workers. This cost factor has undoubtedly been less important in recent decades than previously; since economic opportunity attracts workers. In recent years many employees "have followed the job."

Many industries have been localized as a result of the influence of founders. After these establishments had attained a certain point of development, removal became difficult. Likewise, transportation facilities and labor have been drawn to the particular location. Obviously, certain industries could not be established in areas where a number of unfavorable influences operated. Beyond a doubt, the infant automotive industry could not be established in areas where a number of unfavorable influences were operating, as, for example, in a ranching area. On the other hand, personalities were fundamental in explaining the leadership of Detroit and Flint. If personality factors are excluded, any one of the many Great Lakes cities could have become the automotive capital.

The majority of the smaller cities in the Middle West were characterized by a diversified industrial pattern during the last three decades of the nineteenth century. Representative cities, with a population of between 3,000 and 10,000, had machine shops, foundries, food processing plants, cigar factories, packing houses, printing establishments, breweries, tanneries, agricultural implement shops, and (if not far from sources of supply) furniture factories. The capacity of many of these shops indicates a market beyond the community limits. Late in the century, the establishments in the towns and cities under 10,000 began to operate at a disadvantage in competition with the shops of larger cities. The chair factory with an annual capacity of four hundred units could not compete with the shop in a larger city that produced four thousand units. The later age of specialization often called for a concentration of production of any one commodity in a few, rather than many cities.

Understandably, industrial life has been concentrated in a few of the leading cities. In 1869 Chicago was tenth among the cities in the nation in value of manufactured products.

In 1879 Chicago ranked fourth; in 1899 third; and in 1909 was second. Chicago's rank as the second industrial city of the nation remained unchallenged. The Detroit story is somewhat different. In 1869 Detroit ranked sixteenth. In 1879 it slipped to nineteenth place. In 1899, as it was about to become the automotive capital, the city ranked sixteenth. By 1935 Detroit stood third among the industrial cities.

In 1869 Cleveland was in the nineteenth position. In 1935 Cleveland ranked eighth. In 1869 Milwaukee ranked twenty-first in manufacturing. In 1935 it ranked twelfth. Cincinnati, alone, among the leading cities, declined in industrial rank. In 1869 it was seventh in the nation. By 1935 it had declined to twelfth place.

Americans are daily reminded of their partial dependency upon Midwestern industries. The great meat packing industry has long counted each American family as a consumer. It draws its raw material from several million American farmers. The names of many of the packers are today household words. The processes involved from the receipt of the livestock to the ultimate sale of approximately 200 varieties of sausage and some dozen "cuts" of steak by 400,000 retail outlets are numerous enough to baffle any ambitious compiler of occupational statistics.

Meat packers secure their supplies by sending their trained buyers to the stockyards. Market conditions are constantly fluctuating and must be observed with care and experience. The stock owners in turn usually make their sales through commission men serving as agents.

The stockyards at Chicago came to constitute the chief marketing center. The Chicago techniques and procedures have been imitated by others on a lesser scale. The other major stockyards, distributed on a wide geographic basis, include those in Omaha, East St. Louis, Sioux City, St. Paul, Indianapolis, Cleveland, Cincinnati, and Milwaukee.

The by-products of the packing industry have both an economic and social significance. The edible products such as lard are well known. Approximately one hundred pharmaceutical products utilize some substances derived from the slaughtered animals. Insulin, so effective in the control of diabetes, is derived from the pancreas of hogs and cattle. Cortisone utilized in fighting arthritis and other disorders, is another of the new and now celebrated drugs prepared from the once discarded by-products of the packing house. The products derived from bones range from dice to artificial teeth. By-products utilized by the farmers themselves include animal feed fertilizer. The processing of hides and other industrial commodities, long associated with the meat industry, has become increasingly important as a result of the technological advances of the packers.

We mention here only two of the many personalities who have played an unusual role in the development of the packing industry. Gustavus P. Swift, the founder of the Swift enterprises, started as a butcher's helper in his native Massachusetts and used his savings to establish his own shop. In 1877, he moved to Chicago in order to engage in packing. In Chicago, Swift conceived of the plan of shipping meat in all seasons in refrigerator cars. Many of the railroad people were frankly skeptical. At first the cars were iced before loading and re-iced at major terminals. Some lines substituted brine tanks with ice and salt. Artificial ice-producing machinery, introduced in the eighties, finally solved the problem. Philip D. Armour moved from Milwaukee to Chicago in 1867 in order to secure the greater advantages of the Chicago market. He devised a system of mass production in the butchering of the animal and later introduced the assembly procedure in processing meat and by-products to eliminate waste. Packers agreed that these new techniques enabled them to use everything except the squeal of the prairie hog.

The importance of the earlier export market stimulated the discovery of new methods of canning and curing meats. Some companies specialized exclusively in preparation of canned meats. Machine methods were almost immediately introduced as new processes were developed to supply the unanticipated demand and to reduce costs.

The emphasis given to the major stockyards and packing centers should not detract from the importance of the numerous smaller establishments. Slaughtering houses are found in all except a few of the larger cities. These packing houses often secure their livestock from the nearby farming communities. Many smaller establishments also concentrate upon specialties such as sausages.

The preparation of flour-mill products was also modified by the new industrialism. Minneapolis rapidly moved to the fore to become the capital of this growing industry. The city was adjacent to important wheat growing areas. Likewise, its elevators had huge storage capacities. Of fundamental importance, however, was the introduction of new methods of milling which could better utilize the spring wheat raised in many northern areas. The various new processes of manufacture assured the consumer of a flour richer in food content. New types of mills were also established in the winter wheat producing belts. Kansas City, Wichita, Dallas, Fort Worth, and Oklahoma City were among the new important flour producing centers. Among the cities of the East, Buffalo retained a rank of importance among the major milling cities, primarily because of favorable water transportation and the earlier construction of huge elevators. The hundreds of small flour mills, found throughout all of the wheat-packing areas, demonstrate that the large centers simply did not constitute a monopoly.

Food processing has contributed to the industrial life of many of our cities. Some of the new products have modified the eating habits of the nation. Pioneers in the preparation of processed cereals in Battle Creek, Michigan, and Cedar Rapids, Iowa, were sucessful in manufacturing cereals that soon commanded a national market. The packaged "cracker-jack" is perhaps the best known of the many specialty corn products processed for a large-scale confectionery market.

There was little in the infancy of the automotive industry to suggest that it would be the innovator of mass production. In fact, in the decade of the nineties, in which the automobile was introduced to the American public, we seemed to be more impressed with the bicycle, in so many respects the forerunner of the automoble. By the early nineties, the bicycle was transformed from the awkward high-wheel vehicle, which could be operated only by the skilled, into the graceful chain-driven safety. By the close of the century the bicycle claimed approximately a million enthusiastic riders. An emphasis upon greater speed and additional comfort paralleled the increased use of the contraption. The bicycle had an unusual appeal for townspeople who could not afford to keep a horse. The drawbacks of the bicycle, however, were both obvious and numerous. It accommodated but one person. Worse yet, it afforded no protection from weather. The bicycle was poorly adapted both to rough and muddy roads. Since it was propelled by leg power, it was of service only to the sturdier—mainly the younger—men and women.

The bicycle accustomed many Americans to a freedom of mobility that was ultimately satisfied only by the automobile. Bicycle fans were vociferous in their demands for better roads. The many small-scale manufacturers and mechanics who specialized in tires, wheels, brakes, and other phases of bicycle production and repairs acquired techniques and skills utilized later by automotive people.

The automobile made its first appearance in Europe. In the late eighties, after a long period of exploration and experimentation, an internal combustion engine was finally designed to be used for transportation. In 1893, two brothers, Charles E. and J. Frank Duryea of Springfield, Massachusetts, designed and built the first American horseless carriage. Two years later, the brothers formed the Duryea Motor Wagon Company to manufacture gasoline cars. This company produced thirteen cars over an interval of several years. These pioneers, perhaps because of inadequate capital and lack of manufacturing skill, were unable to become large-scale producers.

Two other brothers, Elmer and Edgar Apperson, of Kokomo, Indiana, also were among the recognized pioneers of manufacturing. In 1895, together with Elwood Haynes, the Appersons undertook the production of the gasoline operated automobile on a very limited scale. Their names, however, are associated only with the early period of automotive industry. In the late nineties, the Pope Manufacturing Company of Hartford, Connecticut, a leading bicycle company, also turned to automotive production. Despite adequate capital, it never became a leading automobile company.

Nevertheless, in spite of countless obstacles these pioneers in the industry were popularizing the horseless carriage. The first automobile race on record was held for Thanksgiving Day, November 28, 1895, in Chicago. The winner attained an average speed of 5.05 miles an hour. The first American automotive trade journal was also published in 1895.

Ransom E. Olds of Lansing, Michigan, was the first American to conceive the idea of manufacturing automobiles on a basis different from the previous pioneers in the industry. In 1891, Olds, whose father manufactured carriages, joined forces with Frank Clark, also the son of a carriage maker.

During the next year, Olds purchased the interests of Clark and relocated the plant in Detroit. To a very considerable extent, the Olds establishment did little more than assemble; since very few of the parts were manufactured in the factory. Olds bought parts from many Detroit companies, previously producing parts for machines, bicycles, and carriages. Because of the standardization and the size of the contract, each jobber concentrated upon the Olds' orders with a consequent reduction in the cost of the product. As a result, Olds could assure both standardization and lower prices. The mechanically complicated Olds sold for approximately $1,250. The company then produced the lighter and less involved runabout to sell for $650. The new model soon attained an unprecedented popularity. In 1902, production reached the 2,500 figure. In the same year, the factory, following a disastrous fire in Detroit, was relocated in Lansing. Detroit suppliers, however, continued to manufacture parts. The public interest in the Olds is indicated by the popular song hit, "In My Merry Oldsmobile." Olds trained many men, in both production and salesmanship, who later attained prominence in the automotive world.

The production of automobiles doubled between 1900 and 1902 with a registered increase from 4,192 to 9,000. This total included both gasoline engine automobiles and electrics. The latter were sold on a limited scale in the cities. The dependence upon a battery for power prevented the electric from attaining any large-scale use. Americans became more accustomed to the automobile in the first two years of the century. In 1900, the first National Automobile Show was held in Madison Square Garden, New York City. In the next year, New Yorkers saw the first motor-driven ambulance. Trucks were in common use in 1902.

In 1903 seventy-eight new concerns were organized to compete with the older companies for the growing automotive market. Of all these companies, the Ford Motor Company was most successful. Ford's interest in the automobile dates back at least ten years before he organized the Ford Motor Company. Henry Ford acquired the mechanical skills attained by the majority of boys reared on a farm in the post-Civil War era. Young Henry left the farm to work in nearby Detroit. In the nineties, Ford, after a varied background in mechanics, was employed as an engineer by the Detroit Edison Company. Ford's first car, which he built in spare moments, attracted little attention. In 1899, however, Ford became chief engineer of the recently organized Detroit Automobile Company in which he owned stock. In 1901 Ford severed his relations with the company, the predecessor of the Cadillac, to found the unsuccessful Henry Ford Motor Company.

Nevertheless, Ford had an adequate background of mechanical and managerial skill when the Ford Motor Company was incorporated in 1903 with a capitalization of $100,000, only $28,000 of which was in cash. During the first year, the company sold only 1,700 cars. In the 1908-1909 year, the sales reached 10,607; in 1910-1911, they mounted to 34,528. In 1912-1913, the company sold 168,304 units. The 1916-1917 figure was 730,041. Sales for the year ending September 30, 1903 amounted to $142,481. The sales for the next year were $1,162,815. Sales rose to $119,489,316 in 1914. The total sales from time of the incorporation of the company to the close of 1921 were almost three billion dollars. These huge gains made Ford one of the most discussed and one of the best-known men in America.

Ford had early acquired a reputation in automotive circles through his patent victory over George B. Selden, who in 1879 had applied for a patent which covered the basic features of the gasoline automobile. Selden had assigned his rights before his patent application was granted in 1895.

The majority of producers were required to pay a royalty. In 1911, Ford was victorious in an involved judicial battle when the courts ruled that Ford, who protested the royalty, was not guilty of infringement. This decision prevented any monopoly in the automotive industry through patent ownership.

Many factors contributed to the Ford success. Although the Ford Motor Company produced different models selling at various prices, the success of the Model T, introduced in 1908, resulted in a concentration of this type beginning in the next year. The first Model T sold for $950, approximately one-half of the average price of other models. By 1915, Ford's mass production methods enabled the company to sell the lowest priced Model T for just under $400. Ford had clearly demonstrated that the public would purchase, in undreamed-of numbers, a car that was within its means.

The Ford name is associated with several other practices. The company was among the first to attain an almost unbelievable goal in the standardization of parts. The company early developed a nation-wide system of dealers who were required to maintain the prescribed standards of service. The company very early began to manufacture the majority of the essential parts instead of purchasing from contractors. This necessitated a continuous expansion of its facilities. The large Highland Park plant was opened in 1914 and in a half dozen years proved to be inadequate. With a decade, the larger portion of the company's manufacturing was carried on in the huge River Rouge factory with its more than 70,000 employees. In 1914, Ford startled the industrial world by inaugurating the minimum five-dollar daily wage scale.

These innovations were initiated or approved by Ford who personally shaped company policies. In 1919, Ford completed the process of purchasing the stock of his associates

to transform the corporation into a family company. He paid
to the original stockholders more than $100,000,000. James
Couzens, who had invested $2,000, sold his share for some
$29,000,000.

The General Motors Corporation also came to the fore
among the early giants of the automobile industry. This
corporation was largely the brain child of William C. Durant,
a highly imaginative man with a quiet "drive," whose business background included experience as a salesman and
carriage manufacturer. In 1904, this carriage company acquired control of a growing automotive concern founded
by David D. Buick. In 1908, Durant believed that the industry could be stabilized by the formation of a company
with sufficient capital to promote a more rapid mechanical
development. Within two years, Durant with the Buick as a
nucleus for the new General Motors, acquired the well-
known Olds, Cadillac, Oakland later called the Pontiac,
and various supply companies. To these companies, he later
added the Chevrolet, incorporated in 1911. Adequate capital
enabled General Motors to undertake research, so vital to
the automotive progress, on a large scale.

Each year, however, the industry announced innovations
to assure greater safety and comfort. Each year, also, the
automobile acquired some features that gradually transformed the one-cylinder horseless carriage into the contemporary graceful and streamlined automobile. The power
tire pump and ignition lock were introduced in 1905. Three
years later, the magnetic speedometer and motor-driven
horns were introduced. Not until 1910 were cars sold on a
completely equipped basis. The 1916 innovations included
the hand-operated windshield wiper, stop-light, and rear-view
mirror. The four wheel hydraulic brake was introduced in
1921 and was the first of many new features of the twenties

that made greater speed possible. The built-in defroster was not developed until 1936.

The automobile has actually modified the behavior pattern of all Americans. The greater mobility afforded by the automobile has appealed to all. The new urban metropolitan area is in large part the by-product of the automotive age. The automobile also virtually ended any basic barriers between town and country.

The new industry created employment for hundreds of thousands of men and women. In addition to the factories, many found work in garages, service stations, salesrooms, and other establishments directly associated with the industry. The automobile has increased in the same astronomical proportions the demand for steel, rubber, gasoline, and, indeed, countless other products.

Manufacturing, accelerated at a tremendous pace by the demands of World War I and World War II, became the dominant industry in several of the states of the Middle West. In 1949 the income derived from manufacturing in Michigan was thirty-nine per cent of the total in comparison with the four per cent contributed by agriculture. In Ohio the figures were manufacturing, thirty-two and agriculture, four; in Illinois twenty-six per cent and five per cent respectively. In Wisconsin manufacturing accounted for nineteen per cent of the income and agriculture eleven per cent. Only in Nebraska, North Dakota, and South Dakota was the income from industry less than ten per cent.

In 1959 Midwesterners were cheered by a new economic potential. The completion of the Great Lakes–St. Lawrence seaway gave the region a seacoast of its own. Chicago, Milwaukee, Duluth, Detroit, Toledo, and Cleveland were among the cities of the Great Lakes to become ports for direct world trade.

The decennial census of 1960 estimated the population of the Middle West at 44,699,000. The following table indicates the comparative figures for 1940 and 1960 for selected states.

	1940	1960
Illinois	7,897,000	10,081,000
Kansas	1,801,000	2,178,000
Michigan	5,256,000	7,823,000
Ohio	6,907,000	7,946,000
South Dakota	697,000	680,000
Wisconsin	3,137,000	3,951,000

The older industrial states made unusual gains as a result of the growth of war industries and the postwar development. Of course, the farm population suffered a drastic decline as a result of the migration to the towns and cities. Consequently, many of the non-industrial countries registered heavy declines in population. The loss, however, was insignificant in countries with one or more industrial towns.

The mood of the Middle West was one of a fortified optimism. The great progress of the area seemed to fulfill the prophetic words of an English writer of the eighteen forties, when the region was in its infancy.

"And now in his place succeeds a permanent population. His old haunts and pleasant ways are trodden by men, who, while they cast a careless eye upon the flying deer, count the resources of every acre which he scorns.

"Broad farms open as by magic on the blooming plain; stately houses take the place of the solitary cabin; and industry, that counts her gains, has stretched her transforming arm over all the fair land. The wild, the free, the mysterious, are fading beneath her touch. But a power is growing up where they vanish, before whose might a continent may tremble. Who shall define the limits of its growth? Who shall conceive what intelligence and moral purpose may do, when they seize upon resources such as these, wherewith to consummate their energies.

"Lands, boundless in extent, exhaustless in fertility, lying under every variety of climate from the tropical to the arctic; accessible in all their parts by continuous water-courses of magnitude unparalleled on the globe, containing so much to stimulate the nobler faculties and gratify the senses; so much that is calculated to induce a high state of physical development and fine perceptions of the beautiful, the grand, and the true; lands whose primeval glory, when it shall have become ancient, will form the theme of the post and glow on the page of the historian; though too feebly sung and written to convey to future ages what the present feels. It must be the theatre of a life larger than human prophecy can foretell!

"When the tide of intelligence shall have swept from the green barrier on the east, to the bald, heaven-reared wall that stretches along the west, and from the northern lakes to the gulf; when the remote tributaries of the great streams shall have become the commercial channels of the vast regions which they drain; and territories equal in extent to empires renowned in history, and surpassing the gardens of the old world in fertility, shall be overspread by a free brotherhood, united as to the great purposes of life, and pursuing them under a liberal and fostering policy—then will be presented the phenomenon of a life, of which we can have now but a faint conception. The pent-up, famishing legions of Europe may find room and abundance here, when they shall have burst the fetters that bind them there! And here may future tyrants behold how great, and good, and strong, is man when left to govern himself; free from want, from oppression, from ignorance, from fear!

"But we are departing from prairie land! The bright

waters of Lake Michigan dance around our steamer. Blue and dim in the distance, fades the mellow-tinted shore, its long faint outline trembling in the golden haze of the Indian summer! Farewell! land of majestic rivers and flowering plains—of fearful storms and genial sunshine—of strong life and glowing beauty! Glorious in thy youth—great in thy maturity—mighty in thy age—thou shalt yet rival the eastern lands of heroism and song, in the worship and affection of man! Thy free plains and far-reaching streams shall be the theatre of a power and intelligence never yet witnessed! Thy countless acres shall glow with checkered beauty and hum with busy life, when the generations of those who love thee now, sleep in thy peaceful bosom! Land of the silent past and stirring future, farewell!"*

* Eliza W. Farnham, *Life in Prairie Land.* (New York, 1847), pp. 407-8.

CHAPTER TWO

The Farm--The Town-- The City

OR THE majority of early Midwestern settlers, agriculture was, of necessity, the fundamental and primary basis of life. For the vast majority, it was the most certain way to make a living. By tilling the soil, any resourceful and ambitious family could produce its own food and other necessities. This self-sufficiency was never a long term goal or permanent condition. As soon as they had overcome frontier conditions, farmers of course produced for a market. The money or goods they received in return enabled them to free themselves, at least in part, from their almost complete dependency upon their own land.

In many respects, the pioneers had to endure lives of toilsome discomforts while they were transforming the previously uncultivated soil into good farm land. Each season brought its problems requiring, frequently, both ingenuity and courage. Although the close of the harvesting period in the North gave some relief from previous burdensome routines, it was a time in which the farmers then prepared for the severe winters. It was necessary, for example, to store fuel for the home and food for the livestock.

During the early years, in order to survive, the entire family had to function as an economic unit. The compensations were an immediate livelihood and, with luck, the accumulation of a little capital for the future. The pioneers derived additional intangible but real values from this laborious rural existence: the amusements and holidays of this almost primitive agricultural life gave a solid satisfaction to those who lived so near to the land.

Forest lands were often transformed into farms by main force and awkwardness. To obtain land with enough sunshine to enable a crop to grow, the settlers had to fell and then burn the trees. Even with a skilled ox team, it frequently was most difficult to break open the soil. The stumps made the work both difficult and endlessly time-consuming; years might elapse before a field was even fairly clear of stumps and stones. Only a few pioneers could afford to own their individual ox team. In general, farmers hired a team; sometimes they paid cash but frequently they worked out the obligation. This first plowing of the cleared land was frequently very laborious. After this plowing, the land was then harrowed. The settlers soon discovered that wheat and corn were excellent early crops to raise on land not previously cultivated.

The settler usually sowed his seed by hand. Skillful farmers discovered that a crop of clover was a good method of preparing the soil for their later standard wheat crop. Farmers discovered and reported that this clover crop might increase their wheat crops as much as five bushels an acre.

Usually, farmers tried as early as possible to grow their own livestock. Although many pioneers could afford only scrub cattle, as promptly as they could they introduced better breeds and selected them to be either beef or dairy cows. Whenever it was possible, the cattle were pastured on timber lands. As they did in colonial days, cattle learned to care for themselves. Hogs also promptly learned to shift for themselves.

Sheep were profitable in a frontier area and, with care, were profitable even in developed communities. Indeed, wool became a favorite cash crop in large areas. Horses are less self-sufficient than most animals in obtaining their food, and must have their special pastures. For this simple reason, many settlers were at first indifferent to the horse; at least they were content to raise ordinary horses without regard to breed. But as they passed the frontier stage, American farmers began to import and breed specified European horses for special purposes.

In general, farmers became and remained heavily dependent upon cash crops. Of these cash crops, wheat was the most general and the most important; secondary cash crops varied a good deal from area to area. Many farmers were so anxious to obtain immediate cash that they sapped the original fertility of their land with never a thought for the soil exhaustion of which we are today so conscious. But we must remember that no pioneer could survive except as an almost self-sufficient operator. He had to keep his immediate needs at a minimum to maintain himself. He even made his own fences out of the wood and stone he found on his farm.

Perhaps we can obtain a more vivid picture of the farmer's problem if we discuss in some detail his major crop—wheat. Wheat can be grown almost anywhere within our Midwestern boundaries. Also, it can be produced with little equipment. Our climates ordinarily assure a farmer at least a few bushels per acre. Wheat also has always commanded a good cash market because of the increase in American urban population and the possible export of surplus to Europe.

Originally, wheat was threshed by methods as primitive as those used in sowing and harvesting it. Until the 1830's

most wheat was threshed with an almost prehistoric in-
strument—the flail. The settler spent untold hours in the
winter months threshing with this simple device. In the
pioneer home, corn also was milled with a simple coffee
grinder or some similar standard household equipment. All
of our astonishing machines have saved a large portion of
crops which otherwise might have been lost.

A few years after the initial settlement the amount of
improved land found on any farm varied with the skill and
industry of the owner. Not infrequently, a farm family had
35 acres under cultivation within a decade after its arrival.
This average development of almost four acres a year is
certainly vivid testimony to the industry of the pioneer
farmer. The most skillful farmers, who studied elementary
methods of conserving and enriching the soil, were always
proud to report their increased yields. They early discovered
deep plowing to be a superior new method. In wheat-raising
areas, soil depletion often led farmers to turn to some other
cash crop or to engage more extensively in general farming.
Many farmers raised the same money crops, year after year,
to the present, causing large areas to suffer from serious
soil exhaustion.

A significant phase of the Midwestern agricultural development was the settlement of the prairie areas, which did not
attract large numbers of homeseekers until after 1830. The
apparent disadvantages of the prairies were numerous.
Pioneers wanted timber to build homes and fences, and the
prairies were prairies, not forest areas. The pioneers were
equally intimidated by the absence of fuel for the anticipated cold winters. They believed that livestock would lose
some of the protection that the woods afforded. The diffi-
cuty of securing a sufficient water supply seemed to be
another serious obstacle. Worst of all, they assumed that it
would be difficult to plow the land.

This final problem was solved when the prairie-breaking plow was developed with a curve in its mold board that actually turned the sod. Farmers soon discovered that they could raise corn during the first year. This in turn enabled them to raise hogs on a large scale. Almost at once, packing houses were erected in some of the leading cities and became marketing outlets for the farmers. In just this manner the newly developed prairie corn belt caused the spectacular development of Chicago as a packing center. During the pioneering years, the prairie farmer could also raise wheat with real success. Fortunately for the prairie farmers, America was generally ready to absorb their products in the astronomical quantities with which they produced them.

The prairie thus offered the advantage, within a short time, of the raising of a staple crop, and consequently stimulated the rise of commercial farming. New machinery, especially the famous reaper and the new plow, made possible this rapid settlement in the prairies. A relatively large portion of the new farms was actually under cultivation after three years. Many regarded this as ample compensation for the lack of timber, the sometimes unfavorable weather, and soil erosion.

Advances in transportation, especially those resulting from railroad construction, accelerated settlement in all the prairie regions. The usual geographic factors were also important in determining a future home site in the prairies. The few wooded lands usually commanded a premium. In turn, many farmers soon moved from their new prairie homes to points even farther west. Iowa and Minnesota attracted hundreds of farmers from the prairie counties of the old Northwest. A large number of the immigrants who turned to agriculture in the forties and fifties sought prairie homes.

In the early pioneering days the new Midwestern farm communities could not readily incorporate advanced knowledge of agriculture. Restricted capital was a barrier from the very beginning and made necessary for many years the purchase of cheaper brands of livestock. Pressure for production forced many Western settlers to neglect good husbandry. They were just unable to give much attention to the problem of soil exhaustion. Their scanty equipment cut down their efficiency. In its general physical appearance the pioneer farm was too often a picture of neglect. The crudely constructed buildings and the absence of orderly fences invariably made a poor impression upon visitors from the older East.

In the years immediately preceding the Civil War, Midwestern agriculture, in general, made significant technical advances. Mid-century farmers began to see in their soil a great wealth potential.These gains indicated our farmers were overcoming the adverse factors that had previously hampered them. The new transportation facilities enabled the farmers to ship both to the overseas markets and the rapidly expanding American cities. This in turn made further specialization possible. For many years farmers had been almost entirely financially dependent upon the local markets. Although in one sense some cities comprised a better market than others, transportation limitations still cut down the farmer's ability to select among markets. After the middle of the nineteenth century, the technological device of the telegraph helped to standardize farm prices.

Wisely, many farmers consciously applied the newly recognized principles of husbandry. The industry accepted the leadership of men who advocated these new techniques to make farming a more profitable and agreeable operation.

Very gradually a large number of Midwestern farmers sensed the advantages of machinery. Many new implements were the result of conscious efforts of American manufacturers to build something which could be used in new markets. Some new implements were regularly invented to enable the farmer to operate his farm successfully under conditions that were quite unknown to the colonial farmer.

Every area apparently could claim credit for improvement in plows. The most striking improvements were made possible by the substitution of iron for wood. There were new plows even for sub-soil plowing. New cultivators were genuine improvements in our American farm equipment. Various rakes, including the hayraker, greatly increased the efficiency requirements of all our American farmers.

The greater emphasis given to wheat stimulated the development of new farm machines to raise this specified crop. Both Europeans and Americans attacked the problems of inventing a machine to cut the grain. Cyrus McCormick patented his reaper in 1834 and is usually given credit as the inventor of this celebrated machine. Until 1845 he did not produce even fifty machines a year. Then, in 1847 he decided to locate in Chicago to reach the expanding prairie market. By 1860, his factory in Chicago was manufacturing 4,000 reapers every year.

The development of the threshing machine was in many ways spectacular. Although the first threshers were introduced early in the century, they were not extensively used until 1840. The machines, constantly improved, originally were operated with horse power. The internal combustion gasoline engine was invented after the Civil War and was promptly used on threshing machines. The threshing machine enabled the farmer to sell his crop immediately after the harvest, reduced his losses from spoilage, and gave him greater flexibility in the choice of markets.

At this time, skillful farmers began their conscious efforts to improve the soil, their primary capital. Commercial fertilizers were developed in larger numbers. Farmers gave far more attention to the centuries-old practice of rotation of crops.

Few of the advances in agriculture matched the technical improvements in the breeding of livestock. All such technical improvements were first advocated by the most progressive farmers, and then taken up by farmers interested in increasing their own production for new and growing markets. An earlier generation was unaware of these techniques, but shortly even shelter and food were improved.

The interest in obtaining better brands of cattle is clearly indicated by the importation of superior and specialized types of cattle. Even on the average farms, Jerseys and Guernseys began to replace the colonial plain cows. The farmers began to invest in superior breeds of hogs as better returns warranted these larger outlays of capital. New strains of hogs resulted from the importation of famous European and Chinese breeds. A few farmers began particularly to import the famous Spanish Merino sheep to increase their annual wool yields. New types of both horses and equipment enabled farmers gradually to replace the slower ox team.

As secondary crops, apple, pear, peach, cherry, and plum trees were raised. Our native nurseries made many basic scientific contributions. They devised really amazing new techniques in grafting. Our early methods of fighting disease remained so cumbersome, however, that few commercial fruit belts could be recognized in the Middle West before 1860. Farmers became more conscious of the possibilities of new crops and began experiments to find them. The first attempts to raise the sugar beet in some northern states were failures because of defects in processing. Beets were then experimentally fed to the cattle. Mulberry trees were planted on an even larger scale than the sugar beet, but even state subsidies could not enable this crop to prosper.

After the Civil War, Midwestern agriculture very definitely became subject to business methods, calculation, and risks to usher in a great era of commercial farming. Agriculture, both in the newly developed and older areas, assumed an economic character different from that of even a generation earlier. Although this trend toward capitalistic farming could be observed in several respects during the first half of the nineteenth century, the speed with which the changes took place baffled many oldsters. The farmer found himself with a number of fixed costs which included machinery, very often interest on debts resulting from the large capital requirements, higher taxes (especially in new communities), and larger cash outlays for personal expenses. Most important of all was the fact that the former high degree of self-sufficiency of the farm had disappeared. To be sure, the average farm family raised most of its food products. Yet, more and more commodities were purchased from the grocery as wilderness game became no longer available. In many areas, the land no longer supplied the wood for fences. Many of the new farms were in the prairie country which lacked many of nature's gifts, so commonly found in the wooded lands. Frequently, farmers could secure an adequate supply of water only by digging deep wells. Unlike the earlier years, a relatively large acreage was placed under immediate cultivation to secure the necessary dollars. Although modern technology made possible a new large-scale farming, modern technology also required large-scale investments. As a result, the farmer in the period of capitalistic agriculture added up the possible expenses, tried to determine his fixed costs of production, and calculated his profits accordingly.

Factors that had never previously played the same significant roles became important. Naturally, the market assumed a position of utmost significance. A low price could now ruin a farmer. Both the local and national market prices could make or break a farmer. Marketing facilities became matters of concern. Transportation costs were often determining factors in explaining a successful season.

Soil conditions, the scientific selection of seed, and climatic factors were taken into consideration by a farmer. No longer could he afford to allot a few acres to unprofitable specialties. Many farmers in wheat areas abandoned experimental orchards in order to attain a maximum return.

Unfortunately the farmer did not know his financial standing until the close of the year. Crop failures or low prices might place him in an unfavorable position. Successive lean years might result in the loss of a farm. Unlike other business people, the farmer had no control over total expenditures. He could do little to lower his cost of production. He knew little about the factors bringing on over-production. Likewise, it was difficult for a farmer to shift to other crops in an age calling for specialized mechanization and markets.

Obviously conditions were most uncertain in staple crop regions. Wheat became an unusually important staple crop in the North. Wheat was naturally a favorite in the newly developed areas, since it commanded a large market. At the same time, the price of wheat was determined in part by a world market. Countless additional factors were included in the establishment of its price for any one farmer. Yet, the number of staple crop farmers especially in the wheat belts increased by many thousands in the years following the close of the Civil War.

This tremendous post-Civil War agricultural expansion resulted in consecutive years of over-production. These surpluses could not be easily anticipated. Good harvests in any one year aggravated the problem. Improved techniques of farming also added to the output. The creation of new farms annually also increased the agricultural products available for sale.

American agriculture had two markets: the export and the domestic. The former was highly unreliable for producers of grain and livestock. Europeans restricted their American purchases except in periods of war and crop failure.

The greater portion of the agricultural output was necessarily sold to the American market. Agricultural productivity, however, increased at a ratio far above that of the population. Huge surpluses of the commodities which lacked the export market frequently depressed the prices. American farmers became increasingly aware that they were frequently producing more than could be consumed. Layman often have suggested that farmers could have solved their problem by shifting to crops for which there was a greater demand and a better price. This solution was too often impossible because of the huge investment in machinery which could be used only for one commodity. Likewise, a farmer could not raise a crop for which his area had no marketing facilities. Farmers also pointed out that some crops could not be raised easily in certain areas where climatic conditions were unfavorable. For example, wheat was the most advantageous crop for any area which was experiencing the frontier stage of development.

The national gains in the agricultural output were not exclusively the result of the cultivation of more land. Between 1870 and 1914, the output of the average farm laborer more than doubled. A considerable portion of this increase must be credited to the mechanization of the farm.

We should not assume that all farmers immediately turned to mechanization. Until late in the last century, many farmers had insufficient capital to purchase more than the very minimum of equipment. Other farmers, even with means, were slow in abandoning traditional and time-honored methods. In fact, in some areas, the new implements came into general use very slowly. Likewise, machines for some farm processes were not invented until this century. We undoubtedly overemphasize the completeness of farm mechanization by generalizing on the basis of the first machinery manufactured for use on staple crop farms.

In the seventies and eighties, much of the new machinery required the use of the horse. The very fact that the farmer could substitute the horse for human labor is in itself significant. Late in the nineteenth century, the gasoline engine became the unusual basis of farm power. This advance, in turn, was followed by gradual electrification in the twentieth century.

Ultimately, few farmers could resist, or afford to resist, the happy combination of new machinery and new sources of power. By 1914, machines had been invented for practically each major process in farming. Since the machine could be most effectively utilized on large farms, the new technology intensified the trend of large-scale farming. The dependency upon technology also made the farmer more conscious of his fixed expenses. Mechanization also encouraged a profitable specialization. Many of the earlier problems of farm labor were eliminated by machinery. In 1860, the labor of the entire family was required in the operation of a 160-acre farm not completely cleared. Three-quarters of a century later, a farmer in his late middle age could supervise 640 acres. All machinery, which was constantly modified and improved, could be easily operated. The machinery and gadgets freed women and children for many other tasks.

The invention of machines to facilitate the harvesting of wheat constitutes a landmark in the development of large-scale farming. The mowing machine and reaper, widely employed at the outbreak of the Civil War, cut the grain and raked it. The binding, however, performed by hand, remained a slow and laborious task. In 1858, two brothers, C. W. and W. W. Marsh of De Kalb, Illinois, perfected the Marsh Harvester, a machine on which men could ride and bind the wheat as it was delivered to them. Wire binders, invented in the early seventies, further simplified the task of harvesting grain. The expensive wire, however, often damaged the threaders. Worse yet, pieces of wire, which were frequently caught in the grain, annoyed the millers. The twine binder, perfected in 1878 by John Appleby of Palmyra, Wisconsin, overcame these defects. Within a few years, several companies were marketing the mechanical self-binders which enabled one man and a team of horses to perform the work formerly required of twenty men. By the close of the century, farmers in the wheat belt were using combines that cut, threshed, and bagged the wheat.

Invention also made possible a larger corn acreage for farmers of the livestock belts. Until the middle of the nineteenth century, corn was shelled by scraping the ear over the edge of a shovel. This bottleneck was broken by the development of the mechanized corn sheller which was rapidly improved to include devices separating the cobs and the kernels. Late in the century, time-saving corn husking machines and corn binders became standard equipment. With the advent of modern and rapid silo-filling equipment, the farmers in the corn-growing states had the advantages of mechanization in all fundamental processes in the production of this basic crop.

Machines were invented for other important phases of husbandry. The potato planter, which first prepares the seed to any specification devised, also drops the seed, covers it, and later fertilizes it with a skill greater than that of the best-trained potato farmer of the early nineteenth century. Potato-digging machines have reduced the harvesting period on a farm from two weeks to a matter of hours. Spraying machines have salvaged major orchards. Even dairying was invaded by the invention of the electric milker and the electric separator. Machines have been manufactured for cleaning and splicing truck crops such as carrots.

Outstanding among the new farm equipment was the gasoline-powered tractor which was more practical and efficient than its less well-known predecessor, the steam tractor. The light and easily operated gasoline tractor is moderately priced because of mass production. The tractor not only performs many tasks but also is used by many farmers as a substitute for a truck.

Scientific agriculture contributed to the improvement of the farm picture. In spite of the many previous advances, the true age of scientific farms begins with the era after the Civil War. Although scientific husbandry was promoted by several factors, the new role of education undoubtedly is the most significant single influence. The training of a new type of farm leader was assumed by the agricultural colleges, which in some instances have become the equivalent of state universities. These institutions, which have broadened their scope in the twentieth century through an extensive program of extension classes, pioneered in many areas of research. Successful experiments with new types of seed enabled farmers to raise crops which it was previously assumed could not be produced because of climatic conditions. The schools have devoted an unusual amount of effort in encouraging farmers to improve their livestock. The intensive research in veterinary science courses did much to abate the epidemics which were the leading sources of insecurity to dairy farmers.

The schools also trained many future leaders of a new rural society. Courses in agriculture in the high school helped train future farmers. The agricultural journals have likewise been of importance. Although the farm press became more specialized than in the pre-Civil War period, the range of technical information has increased. Many of the editors encouraged specialization. The thriving Wisconsin dairying industry must acknowledge its debt to Willams Hempster Howd who devoted a lifetime to the encouragement of dairying. In 1885, he began publication of *Howd's Dairyman,* a weekly which informed its readers of all of the many necessary steps prerequisite for successful dairying. Companies selling to farmers also engaged in research. Nurseries undertook research projects on huge experimental farms. Chicken hatcheries called attention to the value of pedigree. The farm societies have also played a role in promoting scientific husbandry. Farm Institutes were held annually in many states. The programs ordinarily called for a two-day session in which farmers attended lectures and demonstrations. Often the Institute was the feature of a town or a country fair in which farm exhibits were displayed.

Government aid to agriculture has been highly significant since the Civil War. A commissioner of agriculture was authorized in 1862. In 1889, Congress created the Department of Agriculture which was helped and headed by a secretary with Cabinet status. The functions of the Department were expanded each decade. The many publications, which covered a wide range of subjects, were available to farmers throughout the nation. The early policy of distributing certain types of seed free was enlarged. The extension of weather report service to the rural areas represents further evidences of the concern of the federal government for the welfare of the farmer. The Smith-Lever Act of 1914 was the first of many measures that gave aid to local school districts desirous of improving their courses in husbandry.

State governments have increased the scope of their departments of agriculture. Virtually all of the states gave some special attention to high school courses in agriculture. A number of states have also created the office of county agent. Some states have engaged in soil and seed testing. Others supplement the services of the commercial nurseries. State departments have encouraged specific farm industries, such as dairying, by demanding standards that would assure better markets.

The fortunes of farming have varied considerably since the Civil War. More large-scale farmers came to the fore than in the period preceding the Civil War. Another large segment of farmers had only modest holdings that gave them a substantial income. Many of these entrepreneurs were successful because they raised specialized crops. Others were fortunate to be the owners of unusually fertile soil. The growth of nearby towns and cities was a boon to thousands of farmers who were consequently able to specialize in dairying and truck crops. Proximity to a city frequently resulted in an increase of land values.

Thousands of farmers, however, never quite attained success in their occupation. Large-fixed costs of operation and mortgages led to their undoing. Unfavorable climatic conditions or successive years of low prices harmed others. Not a few started with inadequate capital. Others made brave but futile attempts to cultivate sub-marginal land. After years of failure in cultivating poor soil, thousands finally migrated to towns and cities with a scarcity of labor.

The general farm laborer remained a fixture in rural areas. Although many were young "hired men" who worked only a few years in order to save for the purchase of a farm, others were men with families. In many communities, the farm laborer enjoyed a relatively high standard of living. The twentieth century gave rise to another laborer—the migratory worker. These migrants were usually found in staple crop areas. Unlike the general farm hand, the migratory laborer, who usually performed specific tasks, worked with others in a team under supervision.

Modern agriculture is characterized by an unusual emphasis upon specialization. Even the general farmer found it advantageous to concentrate upon fewer commodities than did his grandfather. Although specialization avoided many of the pitfalls of general farming and simplified the task of farming, it also created new ills. Fundamentally, the problem was one of carrying "all eggs in one basket." Specialization required increased mechanization and greater cash expenditures. Far too often, falling prices left an irreparable toll. The farmer found it more difficult to adjust to the uncertainties of specialization than did the manufacturer. Likewise, the dependency upon marketing facilities and the emphasis upon grading and standards made necessary constant and annoying adjustments.

Much of the specialization, which represented judgments based both upon experience and upon a consideration of scientific principles of husbandry and economics, has followed regional lines. The older states of the Middle West stressed, to a degree, a pattern of diversified farming with a new and shifting emphasis upon specialties. This specialization included dairying, truck farming, and poultry farming—all undertaken to supply the growing urban areas. As a result, the farm income has remained relatively stable. The majority of the farms are operated by owners with a minimum of additional farm labor.

The prairie belt constitutes the staple crop region of the North. This belt was a leading producer of wheat and corn. Prairie farmers were subject to many hazards, including insects and blights. Uncertain weather conditions constituted another obstacle. Usually the farms were of a larger size than found elsewhere in the North. Mechaniza-

tion was undertaken on a large scale. Here also one finds
the disastrous consequences of agrarian overproduction.
Because of a scarcity of labor, it was necessary to rely upon
the migratory farm worker. Business practices were taken
into consideration to assure success. By the turn of the
century, Minnesota, North Dakota, South Dakota, and
Kansas were among the six leading wheat-producing states
of the nation. Iowa, Kansas, and Nebraska were the leading
corn states. Although these basic crops were still grown
extensively in other states, the acreage given over to the
production both of wheat and corn usually registered only
a slight increase, if not an actual decline, elsewhere. The
wheat states served as the basis for the great milling industries of the Middle West. Corn-raising was associated
with livestock. Many farmers purchased beef cattle in order
to fatten them for the market while others were engaged
in dairying. The corn raising produced this commodity
primarily to serve as feed for the hogs.

"Hard work," versatility, and patience remained essential
qualities in the almost always trying years that accompany
farming. Only the robust could engage in agriculture. The
larger number were the native-born who, with few exceptions, had been raised on a farm. The rural life was theirs
by choice.

Thousands of European immigrants, mainly with a rural
background in the homeland, also sought new homes in the
Middle West. A large number received lands on the very
fringe of settlement. In 1860 immigrants comprised eleven
per cent of the population of pioneer Kansas. By 1860, the
Scandinavian influence was already noticeable in Illinois,
Wisconsin and Minnesota. German farmers had introduced
new techniques of dairy farming in Wisconsin. Dutch
customs could be observed in several of the counties in
Michigan, Wisconsin, and Iowa.

The states competed for the immigrant population by sending agents to Europe and by maintaining representatives at New York and other major ports of entry. The land grant railroads were equally aggressive. In the eighteen seventies the Chicago, Burlington, and Quincy sent representatives to Russia, Germany, France, Sweden, and Poland to advertise the many advantages of the lands in Nebraska and Iowa. By 1890, the states and railroads had virtually ended their campaigns to attract immigrants.

Apparently, country life has never been a major source of discontent for Midwestern farmers. Their relative proximity to the many trading centers prevented them from experiencing the extreme isolation so frequently associated, especially by urban residents, with the farm. The farmers of the Middle West also rapidly accepted new developments in technology that would add to their comforts. Many farmers subscribed to the view that electricity was cheaper and more effective than hired labor.

World War I was, of course, a turning point in the story of Midwestern agriculture. An enlarged agricultural output became a necessity. State agencies assisted farmers in planning for a larger acreage. Town and city people were trained to serve as farm laborers. The women who volunteered for this service were known as—and the term was not always employed kindly—farmerettes.

The scarcity of wheat, resulting in part from a 1916 crop under the average, induced Congress to create a Grain Corporation with the authority to purchase wheat and to stabilize prices, but not at a price below two dollars a bushel. The agency established the 1917 price at $2.20 and guaranteed $2.26 a bushel for 1918. Farmers responded to the guaranteed wheat price by increasing their acreage. In many countries this increase averaged some fifty per cent.

This new farm prosperity was brief. Agriculture was the

one major industry unable to voice optimism during the twenties. In fact, at the peak periods of prosperity farm spokesmen were often demanding relief for their industry. Although many farmers reported high incomes, other thousands, in particular the farmers in the wheat belts of Kansas and the corn belts of Iowa, complained that their returns were highly inadequate. The figures for farm income, however, clearly reveal that the industry as a whole did not share in the prosperity.

In no one year of the twenties did gross farm income match that of 1919 when farmers enjoyed an immediate postwar prosperity. The year 1921 was very disastrous for Midwestern farmers with net income at a very low point. The total gross farm income, total farm production expense, and net income from farming remained relatively stable between 1925 and 1929. The major gains were recorded during the late twenties when farmers increased production to compensate for lower prices. This in turn added to the surplus.

Farmers were especially alarmed about prices because of the growing debt structure. The debts not only added to the fixed expenses but also forced the farmer to live in fear of foreclosure. A portion of the farm indebtedness represented purchase of additional land, obviously at higher values than previously, in the boom years, 1916—1919. In 1920, Iowa farm land, valued at one hundred dollars an acre in 1910, often was sold for three hundred dollars an acre. Additional indebtedness, however, resulted from the greater mechanization of the farm. The greatest advantage to the average farmer resulted from the purchase of a tractor to replace horses and mules.

Farm machinery was devised or improved to do almost all of the farm tasks. To many of the oldsters the electric milker seemed to be more of a marvel than the tractor. The technological invasion of the farm was as significant as the technological invasion of other industries—and sometimes even more so. Farm labor became less important; the size of individual farms under operation increased; and farmers had fewer tedious tasks. Efficiency was counterbalanced by a greater dependence than previously upon prices to assure a profit.

Not all advances were confined to machinery. Agricultural colleges continued their efforts to find sturdier and more productive seed. The improvement of silos assured farmers a better supply of feed for the livestock.

Farm life was subject to many changes. Naturally, machinery ended some of the drudgery and increased the leisure hours. The greatest benefits were derived, however, from the end of rural isolation made possible by the automobile and radio. Although strides were made in rural electrification, these gains were never geographically uniform.

Throughout the twenties the majority of Midwestern farmers were frustrated by depressed market prices. In 1930, 1931, and 1932 they faced the prospects of a further decline in prices and actual foreclosures. Although the early months of 1933 marked a low point in the morale of the nation, for many of the Midwestern farmers it was a moment of almost complete despair.

The many and intricate New Deal policies designed to relieve the plight of agriculture can be mentioned only in summary fashion. The New Deal attempted to ease the immediate burden of credit in order to give debt-ridden farmers further security. Easier credit, however, was only a portion of the problem, for credit was of no long-term help without a rise in farm prices. The Administration believed that any program of assistance must of necessity also include relief for sub-marginal farmers and the unemployed farm laborers in order to save farm communities. As a result, the problems of agriculture became both economic and social.

Yet, credit alone could not restore agricultural vitality. The New Deal attempts to increase the farm income and to stabilize the industry were among the most discussed and controversial of the Roosevelt policies. The Administration early adopted a program for lowering the total national agricultural output as a means of reducing the surpluses. Also, the Administration guaranteed a minimum farm income through subsidies as a means of compensating for the decreased yield. Obviously, the established government price would become the minimum price. If the formal market prices rose above this figure, the individual farmer would gain from the increase. The agricultural program outlined by the New Deal called essentially for government planning to establish both the level of production and prices. Out of the problem of determining the latter grew parity, the price a farmer should receive in order to give him a return commensurate with the prices he pays for industrial goods and services. Although the parity price theoretically was sufficient to meet the fixed costs of production, Congress outlined the specific limits. As a result, farm prosperity became subject to political and congressional deliberations.

The major agricultural programs were often of little help to small-scale sub-marginal farmers ineligible to enter into farm contracts. The government purchased considerable amounts of inferior land and converted them into recreational areas. It also sponsored a few resettlement programs, but these projects were far from satisfactory. The reduction in average crop cultivation in the larger farms also gave rise to farm unemployment. In spite of the various Administration programs, too often the results merely added to the numbers on the relief rolls.

CHAPTER THREE

Some Midwestern Images

MIDWESTERNERS enjoyed spirited political contests. They participated actively in politics at the grass roots level. Each community exercised its right of self-government by voting on "anything." Frontier people exercised as much control as possible over government. Election days were among the few real holidays on the Midwestern frontier.

Before the era of modern national parties, politics was largely personal. Strong men, with loyal followings, dominated the scene.

With the formation of the Democratic and Whig parties, the Middle West became a two-party region. The personality of Jackson won many converts for the Democrats. Undoubtedly, many supported the Democrats because the party was the champion of the frontier people. The official Democratic policies of a low tariff, internal improvements under state direction, and opposition to a Bank of the United States perhaps meant less than the friendship expressed for the "common man."

The Whigs, earlier known as the National Republicans, advocated a high tariff designed to promote the growth of manufacturing. This, they argued, would minimize sectional issues and strengthen an independent American econ-

95

omy. They also advocated the construction of internal improvements by the Federal Government. They pledged their support to the Bank of the United States. They maintained that these policies would benefit all classes.

Issues, however, were not necessarily the basis for political affiliation. Each party accommodated itself to as many factions as possible. Many supported the Whigs merely because they did not "like" the Democrats.

On one great issue, however, moral conviction became the basis of political criteria. This issue was slavery. In fact, part of the antislavery movement rested upon religious-humanitarian impulses. Midwestern churches were among the first to attack the system of bondage in which the Negroes were held. Many antislavery people pointed out that slavery was not compatible with democracy. Others attacked slavery because it gave rise to an aristocratic social system.

The antislavery movement, early in the nineteenth century, was given over to some plan of voluntary emancipation. Northern agents visited slave owners in the hopes of securing emancipation. Some antislavery advocates were also proponents of a plan to pay the passage of the freed Negroes to Liberia, the independent republic created in Africa. (Its capital, Monrovia, was named in honor of President James Monroe.)

Although a few thousand slaves won their freedom through the efforts of the early societies, this action did not represent any curb on the institution. In the late thirties, the abolitionist societies, dedicated to the program of destroying slavery, were organized. The abolitionists, who were militant, had their large followings in the Midwestern states. A few of the abolitionists even formed a separate political party; since neither the Whigs nor Democrats would incorporate their demands. As a result, the Liberty Party was created by zealots. It mustered few votes in the presidential contests of 1840 and 1844 for its candidate, James Birney.

Nevertheless, by the middle forties, there was ample evidence that the movement was growing. It received the endorsement of countless new enthusiasts. Although many in the North were unwilling to destroy slavery, they were determined to check its spread. A large number of Northern farmers believed that slavery would result in huge estates and rapid land exhaustion which would deprive future generations of free farmers of good land.

The presidential election of 1844 indicated the growing importance of slavery as a major political question. In this contest, the Democrats were pledged both to the annexation of Texas and the occupation of Oregon while the Whigs indifferently supported the same. Although no party defection took place, many Democrats and Whigs opposed the annexation of Texas.

The slavery controversy was further intensified in the war with Mexico (1846-1848) when David Wilmot, a Pennsylvania Democrat, introduced a measure known as the Wilmot Proviso which would have prohibited slavery in any lands which might be acquired as a result of the war. Although this proposal was passed by the House, it was defeated in the Senate. Antislavery forces, however, demanded the election of Congressmen who would endorse the Proviso. The more moderate antislavery factions in the Democratic party were willing to accept a new formula called popular sovereignty, which maintained that each territory should decide for itself whether or not slavery should be allowed. The advocates of this doctrine insisted that it was a democratic principle which would not offend the South (and would still enable a territory upon attaining statehood to outlaw the institution of slavery).

The future of the vast area including at a later date

California, Arizona, and New Mexico was not settled when the nation turned to the presidential contest of 1848. The Democrats selected Lewis Cass, a champion of popular sovereignty; the Whigs nominated General Zachary Taylor, who was evasive; while the antislavery forces nominated former President Van Buren to head the Free Soil Party, which was a successor to the Liberty Party. The Free Soilers also championed homesteads and other liberal causes.

The nomination of Cass of Detroit was a real compliment to the Middle West. The Democrats were most anxious to carry this section.

The victory of Taylor did not lead to an immediate settlement of the issues involved. In 1850 a series of bills, known as the Compromise of 1850, won congressional approval. California was admitted as a free state while the major concession to the South was a new fugitive slave law which placed the burden of proof upon the escaped freedmen. Many believed that the Compromise marked the end of the slavery bitterness.

Instead, however, the decade of the fifties was marked by a sharp emphasis upon the problem. Throughout the ten-year interval prior to the Civil War, the abolitionist strength increased. *Uncle Tom's Cabin* and other accounts that indicted slavery won many followers. Attempts to enforce the Fugitive Slave Law only aroused many in the North who felt that this legislation represented a maximum of appeasement.

A new crisis came in 1854 with the Kansas-Nebraska Act which called for the organization of two new territories, Kansas and Nebraska, without reference to slavery. Many antislavery people, irrespective of previous political affiliations, were determined to prevent any extension of slavery into new territory. In Michigan, the antislavery leaders decided upon some form of political coalition. The problem, however, was one of unifying elements with many political backgrounds into one harmonious and effective grouping.

In June, 1854, an informal group met at Kalamazoo and completed plans for a mass convention to be held at Jackson on July 6. All antislavery people were invited to attend. Ten thousand signatures were received in response to this call, which made it clear that a united front against the extension of slavery was being organized.

On July 6, 1854, some 1,500 persons gathered at Jackson to take some definite political action. There was no hall large enough to accommodate this assemblage and the convention was adjourned to an oak grove outside the village. Speakers who advocated a new party were given enthusiastic applause. The most important of the thirteen resolutions adopted was the one which said that "we will cooperate and be known as Republicans until the contest is ended." Most of the remaining resolutions were directed against the institution of slavery and methods of restricting its encroachments. No specific abolition of slavery, however, was demanded. A demand for a more economical administration and a request for a general railroad law were the only two resolutions relating to state affairs.

There has been considerable argument surrounding the naming of the new party. A resident of Ripon, Wisconsin, insisted that he wrote to Horace Greeley of the New York *Tribune* in June before the Jackson Convention and suggested the name "Republican." There is little doubt that Greeley mentioned the term to Joseph Warren of the Detroit *Tribune* in correspondence carried on between them in regard to a new party. The Wisconsin Republican Party was not organized until one week after the Jackson Convention. The Republicans now officially recognize Jackson as the birthplace of their party.

The Jackson Convention successfully launched the Re-

publican Party. Undoubtedly very few realized that this
new third party, founded in the year of a congressional
election, would soon become one of the two major parties.

Local groups were formed rapidly in both states and an
enthusiastic campaign resulted. In Michigan the new party
won a complete victory in the election of 1854. Not only
were all of its nominees for state offices successful, but three
out of the four congressional seats were captured by the
Republicans, who also gained control of both houses in the
Legislature. In Wisconsin the Republican nominee for
lieutenant governor was victorious. Two of the state's
congressional seats were also captured by the Republicans.

In 1860 the two leading candidates for the presidency
were Midwesterners. Both Douglas and Lincoln had received
their political training in Illinois. Historians have long
quibbled over the precise stand of each man in the 1860
campaign. In essence, however, the Lincoln supporters under-
stood his position as a defense of the rights of man. Lincoln's
victory must be interpreted as a victory for Midwestern
morality.

Between 1865 and 1900 the Midwestern farmer injected
economic issues into American politics. During this interval
the farmer abandoned his traditional individualism in order
to protect his economic status and way of life against the
encroachments of a growing industrial society whose ways
he did not always understand. His villians varied. Ordinarily, however, railroads and monopolies held a high
priority.

In a sense, farm prosperity was an individual matter to
which many factors contributed. Farmers suffered, as did
others, in the depression periods beginning in 1873 and
in 1893. In the more recently developed wheat and corn
areas, however, the typical farmer experienced many "lean"
years. The effects of the panic of 1873 were not overcome

until late in the decade. Even the prosperity of the next decade failed to restore an economic equilibrium for many farmers. A period of seriously declining prices began several years prior to the crash of 1893. The late years of the decade ushered in a period of favorable conditions which reached its peak during the interval of World War I.

The Panic of 1873 was preceded by several successive seasons that were disastrous to the farmers in the most recently settled areas of the Middle West. Consequently, these farmers began to think in terms of securing a greater return from the dollar. They thought in terms of lower transportation rates. They also obviously desired better marketing conditions. These requests and demands for relief would not have been formulated and emphasized if farm prices had remained high. The farmer in a new age of commercial agriculture found himself in a peculiar position. He now was forced to meet his fixed costs of production not only to satisfy his immediate economic needs but also, in many instances, to save his farm.

The farmer had no background of experience with aggressive organizations as did the laborer. The first agricultural and horticultural societies, which had small memberships, were devoted to the attainment of narrow professional goals. The order of the Patrons of Husbandry, a national secret fraternal order which was known as the Grange, proved to be different from the earlier rural societies. This organization was founded by Oliver Kelley, an employee of the Bureau of Agriculture in Washington, who was instructed in 1866 by President Johnson to tour the Southern states and to report upon their agricultural status. Kelley was convinced, as a result of his journey, that the two sections of the United States did not understand each other. He believed that a national fraternity of farmers might aid in healing the wounds caused by the recent struggle. He felt likewise that the farmers as a class were suffering from ills to which they themselves were indifferent. He accordingly prepared to establish an organization, not confined to the South, that would enroll farmers in a separate association to protect their interests and to promote social and educational projects. The first chapter was established in 1867. Five years later, the order had attained a point of growth that made possible a national session attended by delegates from eleven different states. The term Grange, which means farm home, was used to designate all units of the order. The term is also the more customary designation of the Patrons of Husbandry. The organization of the Grange was sufficiently flexible to make possible the adoption of a policy by a primary or local unit without the consent of the national order.

Although Kelley had intended that the order should eradicate ill-will, the farmers in many Midwestern states seized upon the Patrons of Husbandry as the one medium through which they might obtain relief from certain economic ills prevalent even prior to the time of the organization. The highest ratio of membership was in Nebraska and Kansas. In these two states and in Illinois, Iowa, Wisconsin, and Minnesota the Grangers outlined a reform program, which actually was partially attained. Because of the activities of the Grange in the Midwestern states, the order was often regarded as a political body. This was not true. Ordinarily, the Grange worked with one of the existing parties. The flexibility within the organization made possible action on a county or state basis. During the period of Granger activity, the farmer set out to win control of the legislature in those states where unity could lead to victory. No separate ticket was organized except in a few counties. Some Grangers identified themselves with the new Greenback Party. When political power had been secured, the legislatures, between 1873 and 1876, responded with measures known as Granger Laws. Although these varied from state to state, in general, the state governments were empowered to create railroad commissions and to establish maximum rates. Lower legal rates of interest were authorized by some legislatures. Elevators were likewise brought within the scope of control in a number of ways. State-wide inspection of scales was a by-product of the Grange demands in several of the states. Usually the Granger legislation was also concerned with the promotion of scientific husbandry by the state governments. Both the revival of farm prosperity and the attainment of the major goals resulted in a decline of further legislative demands.

The Grange gradually became the sponsor of cooperatives. Although the pioneer national Grange leaders (who gradually lost influence) did not intend their order as a business agency, the demand for cooperatives increased with the growth of the Patrons of Husbandry in the Western states, where the middleman was under attack. In the face of threats of secession from the organization, the national body finally sanctioned cooperatives. The cooperative program was a fundamental characteristic of the Grange between 1874 and 1879.

Cooperatives for distribution took various forms. Many members were content to rely upon national supply-houses, including Montgomery Ward and Company, which sold directly to farmers by mail. In a few instances the distributing agencies were owned by Grange members.

Frequently state Granges secured the services of a State Purchasing Agent who entered into contracts with dealers to supply specific items to members at a discount. The state agents usually confined their understandings to distributors of plants, seed, basic food commodities, and farm implements.

In 1875, the national order authorized the local Granges, or even a portion of the membership, to form their own retail establishments. Profits were to be used both for fostering additional cooperatives and furthering educational programs. These undertakings resulted in failure. The stores were unable to give credit which was essential in a rural area. If the managers attempted to compete on a basis of equality with a private merchant, they found themselves burdened with the fixed costs of the retailer. Although these retail establishments failed, some Grange cooperatives which were engaged in production, such as dairy establishments, were more successful. Some of the insurance societies were also established on a sound basis.

After 1880, the Grange abandoned the emphasis upon political action and cooperatives. Attention was directed to pure food laws, improvement of rural life, more adequate educational facilities, and good government. Although some states reported a decline in membership, the "Grange Hall" was an important community center in most rural areas.

The general farm prosperity of the eighties was reflected in the numerical weakness of the few organizations that advocated a great rural militancy. Nevertheless, a small minority advocated political action and a great emphasis upon economic reform. The following is typical of the appeal made by agrarian leaders who desired a revival of the more aggressive pattern and spirit of the seventies.

"[Farmers] have seen messages of Presidents covering pages of the daily press and referring to the condition of the various interests and industries of the people, and seldom devoting a dozen lines to agriculture. . . . We neglected to say how much is appropriated annually in support of agriculture, but it does not matter much as it never reaches a million. For this meager representation and this continued neglect—this unfair treatment, the farmers of the country are themselves responsible, are themselves to blame. . . . There are useages that precede elections made necessary for the better concentration of votes upon individuals, and if farmers prepare to look out for themselves better than they have been doing, they must take a hand in this preliminary work. They must consult together and determine upon a line of action, and then pursue it with the same regard to the outcome that they give to any other business where their interests are involved. Don't forget that you are farmers and that the great agricultural interests of the country have been neglected and belittled by Whigs, Democrats, and Republicans alike, in the Congress of the United States. No party, as such . . . has undertaken to amend these laws. . . . We do not ask you to vote only for farmers for all offices, but we ask you to attend the primary meetings of the party with which you have been identified. . . . Resist the schemes of small politicians. . . . Farmers . . . we arraign you as responsible for a condition of things that is a reproach to your intelligence, your business capacity and your independence. You have worked for a party rather than a purpose."*

Comments of this type began to appeal to numerous farmers suffering from the declining income of the late eighties and early nineties. In this new wave of agrarian discontent farmers found numerous vehicles of organization awaiting them. Gradually, the various new societies were welded into two great organizations: the National Farmers' Alliance of the North and the Farmers' Alliance and Industrial Union of the South. Both of these organizations, which sought to increase membership rolls throughout the eighties, encouraged cooperatives, and in other respects, subscribed to the tactics of the earlier aggressive Midwestern Grangers.

---

* *Grange Visitor*, August 1, 1885.

In 1890 the Alliance entered politics, as a third party, in several states. They gained control of the legislatures in Kansas and Nebraska and registered some strength elsewhere. The Alliance elected nine men to Congress.

At a meeting held in St. Louis in February, 1892, delegates from the Alliance joined with representatives from other farm organizations and a handful of labor spokesmen and reformers to lay the groundwork for the National People's Party. The Populists, as the new body was termed, were dominated by the Alliance, which hoped for labor, reform, and inflationist support. The platform, which was adopted at a later convention in Omaha, advocated money inflation both of the free coinage of silver at a ratio of sixteen to one and paper-money issuance. General James B. Weaver, a former Greenbacker, was nominated for the presidency. The Populists also demanded the Alliance sponsored sub-Treasury, a plan whereby farmers could borrow upon food products stored in national warehouses. Government ownership of railroads, a graduated income tax, a postal savings system, and election reforms were among the other planks.

Although the Populists of the Middle West captured Kansas and North Dakota and elected a handful to Congress (with the help of colorful campaigners), their strength was primarily rural. When the Democrats adopted the free coinage plank in 1896, the majority of Populists supported William Jennings Bryan, the Democratic nominee for president. Populism, which lost its identity by this action, was never revived on a successful basis. The movement, which interestingly brought farmers of the North and South together, was the last of the agrarian uprisings of the nineteenth century. It also was the first major agrarian movement to attempt to solve rural problems on a national basis.

William Jennings Bryan was only thirty-six years of age when he won the Democratic nomination for the presidency. Bryan, a native of Illinois who moved to Lincoln, Nebraska, possessed qualities that appealed to Midwestern voters. He was a master of the oratorical art. His memory was phenomenal. He enjoyed the political nickname, "The Commoner," bestowed upon him by his many loyal followers. He was presented to the electorate as a man of and friend of "the people." He oversimplified complicated economic problems and offered understandable political solutions. In his heart Bryan was probably a conservative Populist. In spite of his defeat in 1896, Bryan led the Democrats again in 1900 and in 1908. Although the electoral returns do not always so indicate, Bryan weaned many followers from the Republican ranks.

In the twentieth century the question of government intervention in the economic order became a major political issue. The criticism of monopolies and new business practices had become significant as early as the seventies. These protests ultimately inspired both state and national legislation. Ironically, sponsors of such laws often worked at cross-purposes to bring changes both to assure competition and to provide regulation banning competition. Nevertheless, the cumulative results of movements for reform are reflected in the numerous statistics of laws passed by state legislatures and Congress. As a result, an earlier philosophy of laissez faire implying that government should let business alone was supplemented in part by one imposing greater governmental direction over the economic order.

The attacks upon monopolies stemmed from several forces. In the first place, the anti-monopoly sentiment was a part of the American tradition. Jackson's attack upon the Second Bank of the United States was fundamentally the result of his sincere belief that Nicholas Biddle headed a monopoly. This same attitude was reflected in a rather general distrust of large banking institutions.

Secondly, Americans are anxious to preserve competition. Advocates of regulation can always argue that they are merely attempting to restore or to assure competition. Many adhere to the view that size in itself inevitably leads to domination by the largest corporations. As a result, competition is restricted even if the giants do not consciously intend to bring this about.

Thirdly, regulation is supported by an appeal to fair play. Obviously, unfair practices are not only un-American, but they likewise present competition. President Wilson emphasized this point of view when he sponsored regulatory measures.

Fourthly, regulation is defended as a safeguard to the public. The most common argument is protection from excessive charges. Protection against the use of dangerous or substandard products serves as another reason for invoking legislation.

Finally, dissatisfied stockholders have often demanded legislation. The ruined investors have regularly requested investigation. Protective associations of stockholders have likewise initiated many inquiries.

The direct attacks made against combinations by the reform elements in the many third party or splinter party movements indicate a growing hostility to the new trend. Many of the leaders in the Liberal Republican movement of 1872 were highly critical of monopoly. The subsequent Greenback parties were even more direct in their criticism; and their platforms contained bitter indictments of contemporary conditions. In 1884, the prevailing third party sentiments were directed primarily against the combinations. The former Greenback elements were fused into the

Anti-Monopoly party, and nominated Benjamin Butler for the presidency. Although the support given to Butler was negligible, the mere existence of the party is indicative of a trend. This concentration of attack was sufficiently powerful to result in action by Congress. In the late eighties, legislative committees investigated the trust problem. A Republican president, William Harrison, advocated action against combinations if conspiracy could be shown. The Sherman Anti-Trust Act of 1890 was passed as a culmination of the first reaction against the new trends.

In the late nineties and in the first decade of this century, a new spirit of reform frequently known as progressivism made its appearance. Several factors, including a few that were seemingly contradictory, explain the curious strength of progressivism. In some respects this new trend represented the counterpart of European liberalism with its emphasis upon change and progress. The progressive spirit was in part the outgrowth of American humanitarianism. Specific demands of third parties and labor organizations also were to find places. The spokesmen of progressivism insisted that they were seeking a twentieth-century implementation of American democracy and naturally attacked all forms of monopolies. Some of the progressives, however, directed their criticisms against other phases of the business scene. A few of the writers identified with the progressive school of thought helped, perhaps unintentionally, to create a stereotype of the giant in the business world as an individual indifferent to social ills and frequently successful as a result of unscrupulous policies. Progressives believed that, as a starting point, government should be made more responsive to the people.

Progressivism was promoted by many vehicles. Lecturers carried its tenets to thousands. The most successful advocates, however, were the popular journalists called the muckrakers.

These journalists reached a very wide reading public, including many middle-class people. Although some muckrakers were accused of sensationalism, the majority used an intellectual appeal. Many, however, directed their attack along single lines. The larger number believed that reform in politics, including the substitution of the primary election procedure in place of the convention plan, was essential. Corruption in city government was an almost universal target.

Many of the outstanding Midwestern public servants subscribed to the principles of progressivism. The impressive list of reform mayors included Samuel (Golden Rule) Jones of Toledo who pledged the application of the Golden Rule to his administration; Jones's successor, Brand Whitlock, later to serve as an envoy to Belgium in the critical years of World War I; and Tom Johnson, victor in four bitter campaigns in Cleveland. Albert B. Cummins of Iowa served as governor prior to his election to the Senate of the United States. Robert M. LaFollette, perhaps the ultra-progressive of the better-known public figures, was sent to the Senate of the United States after three terms as governor in Wisconsin. With this array of strength the spirit of progressivism inevitably colored much of our significant legislation. Economic reforms, however, remained crucial. Many reformers demanded only municipal ownership of utilities and services. All of these critics stressed the greater use of the power of government, but not necessarily that of the federal government, to attain their goals.

Theodore Roosevelt was also imbued with progressivism. In 1912 he headed the schismatic Republican wing known as the Progressive Party. Roosevelt carried five states. Three —Michigan, Minnesota, and South Dakota—were in the Middle West. The Progressive vote was also highly impressive in the other Midwestern states. By 1916, however, the new issues of foreign policy and the liberal Wilsonian legislation had crippled the Theodore Roosevelt Progressives. A handful of the Progressives became Democrats, while the rest returned to the Republican fold as "liberals."

Progressivism declined after World War I. By the mid-twenties, however, many Midwestern farmers again sought economic relief.

In the agrarian crises of the seventies and nineties, the farmers formulated aggressive programs of relief and brought political pressure in the hopes of attaining their goals. In the nineteen-twenties, history, with modifications, repeated itself. Two basic differences, however, could be noted, First, the farmers based their hopes almost exclusively upon federal policies to the virtual exclusion of state action. Secondly, agrarian strength was demonstrated by the informal creation of a congressional farm bloc mustered primarily from members of the two major parties. The old Populist notion of independent political action no longer appealed to many. The Non-Partisan League of North Dakota, formed in North Dakota in 1915 by Arthur Townley as a vehicle for political and economic action, the Farmer-Labor Party of Minnesota, and the LaFollette groups in Wisconsin alone constituted major schismatic elements. Several Republican legislators from farm states also failed to follow party lines on many issues. Democratic legislators from cotton states joined Western farmers in making demands for agrarian help.

This new Farm Bloc secured legislation favorable to the farmer. Both in 1927 and in 1928 President Coolidge, however, vetoed the McNary-Haughen Bill, sponsored by the more aggressive agrarian groups. This measure provided for the government purchase of agricultural staples at a government fixed price. The veto left a "bitter taste" with many farmers who felt that the Republican Party was growing indifferent to their welfare.

In 1928 the Middle West was regarded as Republican country. In 1930, as a consequence of the beginnings of the Great Depression, the Democrats made significant inroads. Two years later, in urban and in rural areas, the rate of desertion of Republicans stunned the party leaders. In 1936 the Republicans nominated Alfred M. Landon, the popular Kansas governor, for the presidency. The New Deal recovery program had its appeal. The Republican rout was more complete than in 1932.

After 1936 a new political pattern could be discerned. The two-party system became a long-term reality in each state with independents or switch-voters holding the balance. The rural vote has tended to favor the Republicans. In turn, the Democrats have been dependent upon the so-called "labor vote" in the large cities.

The New Deal era definitely marked the beginning of a new phase of labor history. At the moment of President Roosevelt's inauguration, labor fortunes were at a low ebb. Membership rolls of unions had steadily decreased as a result of the depression. The majority of unions also had insufficient funds to undertake either welfare programs or militant action. In less than a decade, however, largely as a result of friendly legislation, unions accomplished a really vast program of mass organization.

Federal legislation of 1933 assured labor the right to organize. By 1935 the C.I.O. had outlined an aggressive program for industrial unionism. In the Middle West the most impressive C.I.O. victories grew out of the unionization of previously unorganized steel and automotive workers. The C.I.O. did not confine its demands to issues of wage increases; it also included requests for welfare programs and a partial determination of the ratio of production. It entered national, state, and urban political contests. The vast majority of its endorsements has gone to Democrats.

One characteristic of the Midwestern voting pattern has often puzzled political observers. The Midwestern electorate apparently has taken great pride in Senators who have become national figures. These men have been re-elected in the face of almost insurmountable political trends. By way of illustration, Robert Taft of Ohio and Arthur Vandenberg of Michigan demonstrated tremendous strength in their contests for the United States Senate during the thirties.

The spiritual and the cultural were vital in the early Midwestern communities. The large number of rural churches testifies to the pioneers' concern with religion. Although the Midwestern states varied in the degree of support given to education, almost no communities were without some form of elementary school. In these schools the frontier objectives of education were fulfilled. The youngsters were taught to be mannerly and to spell and to speak correctly. Rigid discipline was defended as the best means of developing character. These schools were almost wholly the product of local central and community initiative.

The practical and ambitious Midwesterners were soon to equate education with opportunity and social mobility and good citizenship. Education became a necessity. State support and a greater degree of accompanying state control were accepted. With the increasing financial assistance went a trend toward compulsory education. In 1870 some 136,000 in Chicago were under twenty-one years of age. Yet thirty-eight thousand were enrolled in the thirty-six public schools maintained by the Board of Education. This same significant ratio was not uncommon in other cities of the Middle West.

The free public high school was given early encouragement as a substitute for the tuition-supported academy. The famous Kalamazoo decision, rendered by Justice Thomas M. Cooley of the Michigan Supreme Court in 1874, was of national significance in encouraging secondary education. Justice Cooley upheld the right of the Kalamazoo School Board to use primary school money (state aid funds) for high school purposes.

The state university, with its professional colleges, is the apex of the public education system in each state. Each state supplemented the university by establishing other collegiate institutions which frequently emphasized instruction in husbandry or pedagogy. Many of these institutions have since attained university status. A large number of Midwestern cities have established their own community junior colleges and a few have maintained city colleges or municipal universities.

Denominational collegiate institutions are numerous throughout the entire Middle West. Northwestern University, the University of Chicago, and the University of Notre Dame have sectarian origins. The denominational school is largely the product of the goal that collegiate education should emphasize specific religious ideals.

What is the popular image of the Middle West? Surely, readers of Sinclair Lewis' *Main Street* have gained the impression that the Middle West has a distinct culture—almost a way of life, perhaps. This culture, so void of new or rich ideas, is perpetuated by self-righteous and smug hypocrites. In later life, Lewis insisted that many of his views had been misinterpreted. Gopher Prairie, the fictitious locale of *Main Street,* remains, however, more real to many than any town listed in a state atlas.

Hamlin Garland and Sherwood Anderson also helped to destroy many notions about the good and balanced life in the rural Midwest. The Hoosier-born George Ade used dialect and slang in newspaper columns to strike at many Midwestern attitudes. The poet Vachel Lindsay bemoaned the loss of an earlier Lincolnian idealism. The great social scientist, Thorstein Veblen, expressed scorn for the small town which he described as a predatory institution lacking the homogeneity ascribed to it.

All of these critics were imbued with the spirit of Progressivism in politics. The majority had been influenced by the idealism of the Chautaugua and other public lecturers. Also, these critics presented their demands for social reforms with a reporter's skill. In many instances, they helped to revive or awake a public conscience.

In a sense, however, these courageous men lacked a necessary sentiment or feeling for the Middle West. Carl Sandburg, who has an abundance of love for his native Middle West, portrays the area differently. His dissection of Galesburg, Illinois, is friendly. He has the same affectionate understanding of Chicago. Throughout the rural and the urban Middle West, Sandburg sees the vitality, the friendly tolerance for the many nationality and religious strains, the neighborhood and civic consciousness, and the effort to implement democratic ideals.

The villages and towns that emerged in the recently settled frontier areas were vital to the life of the farmers. Plans for a town were often laid simultaneously with the arrival of the first farmers. This was a common practice when land companies, which often hoped to reap their greatest profits from the sale of town sites, sponsored the farming community in general.

Various considerations, of course, entered into the problem of locating a town. The earliest pioneers tried to settle near rivers, and many of the most prosperous early towns were laid out on favorable water sites with their easier

modes of transportation. Mill power was another basic
determining factor. Just ordinary speculative ownership also
played a part in the establishment of many villages. The
growth of a town was accelerated by the activities of its
own energetic business leaders.

Certain basic services could be rendered only in the
towns. Most of the progressive hamlets had post offices.
The arrival of mail became an important social event in
the days when the schedule was highly uncertain and when
the tempo of village life was monotonous.

The blacksmith frequently earned his greatest cash income as a gunsmith and was usually the most important of
the local artisans. He made and repaired the diversified
equipment needed on the farm. Some smiths were even
capable of producing machines of some complexity.

Mills, of course, varied with the products of the local
farms. Usually an individual grain farmer had enough
wheat converted into flour at the local elevator for his
own use and then sold any surplus. Woolen mills were not
uncommon, and wool was generally a good cash commodity.
Most flourishing towns had their own tanneries, although
often weeks of effort were required to prepare the surplus
hides for export to the larger towns.

As trading increased, the small general store became a
significant mail and business center. In the pioneer era
an energetic individual enterpriser could construct and
stock a general store in the country with a capital of $500.00.
In other words, the establishment of a general store required no more capital than was necessary to start a new
farm in a new area. Almost always the country merchant
was more than a distributor. He had to extend credit to
all of his customers. Inasmuch as cash was chronically scarce
in rural communities, the merchant and his customers
relied partially on barter. The country merchant accepted al-

most all of the products that were raised on the local farms. He usually sent surpluses of farm products which he had obtained by barter to the growing cities. Credit which was usually extended by the country merchant rested, of course, in part upon the credit terms given to him in turn by the wholesaler. The successful proprietor of a general store was genuinely well informed in the marketing of many commodities.

Ultimately further specialization appeared. The hardware store was common to most frontier towns. The taverns continued to cater to the newcomers and to serve as a "special occasion" place for those who wanted an atmosphere of greater luxury than the frontier homes normally could provide.

The village newspapers were unusual boosters. Their columns also indicate the real vitality of commercial life. Advertisements announcing the receipt of new goods from the city testify to the thriving importing and exporting activities; since, even before the railroad era, wagon freight lines and stage coaches linked the major cities and the interior towns.

Specialized manufacturing establishments promptly appeared in almost all enterprising towns. Although some craftsmen came from the East to pursue their former skills, others migrated without definite plans. Each community tried as far as possible to free itself from a dependence upon articles transported a great distance at, sometimes, all but prohibitive freight costs.

From these pioneer centers emerged the well-known and well-publicized twentieth-century Midwestern "Main Street" communities. Throughout all of the rural Midwest, the hamlets and small towns served as the significant economic-social centers. The former with a population ranging from forty to one hundred inhabitants was ordinarily within walking distance of all of the few hundred individuals comprising this unique neighborhood. Often these distribution points were little more than sidings usually found at convenient intervals along one of the numerous railroad lines. Each state also had its prosperous inland centers. The representative hamlet most frequently included a country store, a general produce agent, a blacksmith, a mason, a carpenter, a country school, a church, and in rare instances, a physician and a veterinary. This community was characterized by a peculiar social homogeneity, almost alien to urban people.

The rural town, on the other hand, was a more elaborate trading point which rendered economic and professional services ordinarily not available at the hamlet. Farmers, with the exception of those few living immediately adjacent to the town, limited their town visits to Saturdays, circus days, fairs, homecoming, or some distinctive shopping day. These villages or towns with populations of from three hundred to some two thousand were really very important as economic units. The presence of a substantial number of modern stores contributed to the business life. The most thriving towns could boast of several groceries, two or more general stores, hardware establishments, and meat markets. Ordinarily, the hamlet lacked a hardware store and a meat market. The inventory of its general store also represented a smaller investment than that of the merchant in the town.

Towns ordinarily had additional places of business that distinguished them from the small open-country business centers. Confectioneries and bakeries, or the combination of the two, were usually located in the larger towns. A pharmacy was almost a fixture in towns and was almost never present in the hamlet. Banks serve as a further index in distinguishing the village from the hamlet.

Professional services rendered by the town were both

numerous and vital. The physician was found in all towns. In fact, towns with a population of more than 500 usually had several medical men. Each town was also the home of a veterinary. Attorneys were also prominent among the professional people of the town. The lawyers served frequently also in the capacity of realty and insurance agents. The skilled services provided by the shoemaker and the dressmaker in the town were almost absent in the hamlet.

Prominent in most towns were auctioneers, insurance and real estate agents—often combined—representatives of national concerns, and music teachers. The weekly newspaper emphasized personal and economic activities. In every respect, the town as distinguished from the hamlet afforded a variety of cosmopolitan services. The post office was always a busy center and popular meeting place. Produce agents assured the farmers a good market. All of the towns had small hotels, boarding-houses, and restaurants. County seats and railroad junctions could ordinarily boast a number of well-known restaurants.

In many ways life in the towns and villages was distinguished from that of the city. One of the outstanding differences was the greater community compactness. The individual was less anonymous than in the city and acquired a greater security. The small town, however, made certain demands of comformity with which we are all familiar. Families in the lower economic brackets were never denied a place of some equality in the social life. Gross immorality erased the good standing even of the wealthiest.

The business people in the towns were well aware of the importance of the adjacent farming community. Every inducement was made to encourage farmers to increase their number of shopping days. Prior to the advent of the automobile all main streets had hitching posts and drinking fountains for the horses. Fairs and homecoming days usually united the farmers and townspeople and called attention to the real community of interests.

With few exceptions the advent of the automotive age resulted in the disappearance of the hamlet. The older generation sometimes bemoans the death of these "four corners" community centers. On the other hand, the town gained as a result of the automobile. Also, because of the automobile, towns were better able to integrate farmers into their community activities.

The city was not the frightening and mysterious place that its many critics so often assumed it to be. At the same time, the tempo of life in the city inevitably differed from that of the town and the country to a degree that invited rural suspicions. The dynamic character of our leading Midwestern cities was merely an expression of forces operating with great power. Urban sophistication was often the compensation for a degree of anonymity shared by all urban people.

Our large Midwestern cities were almost destined to become great urban cities. The rapid rate of growth began even before the Civil War. In 1830 Chicago, not incorporated until 1833, had seventy inhabitants. In 1850 the population was 29,000. During the same two-decade interval the population of Cleveland increased from 1,000 to 17,000. During these twenty years the population of Detroit increased from 2,200 to 21,000. Cincinnati, a well-established metropolis of 24,000 in 1830, had a population of 115,000 in 1850.

The attractions of the city have been many. Large numbers moved to the cities merely because they enjoyed cosmopolitan life. Others settled in cities because of occupational training. The most specialized of our artisans could earn a living only in the largest towns. Unskilled workers were reasonably certain that a large city could utilize their services. In spite of opportunities on the rural frontier many lacked the general training required for frontier farming. The city was their only hope.

Understandably, men with mercantile interests flocked to the cities. A scarcity of capital in new and growing cities placed a real premium upon wealth. Professional men believed that their talents could best be utilized in cities. Many went to cities because they desired to live an anonymous life. The city was a refuge for men and women who wished "to start life over again."

Undoubtedly, the chief stimulus for the growth of cities was the great increase in industrial activity. As we have mentioned, the post-Civil War industrial pattern required a degree of concentration. The pool of reserve labor was another factor of importance. Cities also had adequate diversified commercial interests. As a result, many cities were commercial centers of importance, manufacturing was ordinarily an important adjunct of the economic life.

Our large cities always numbered among their citizens a group of men determined to promote their growth in population and their industrial expansion. In other words, cities developed because they took the initiative in stimulating their own growth. This energetic citizenry often represented diversified commercial interest. As a result, many cities were fortunate in securing a diversified economy.

This vitality and confidence can be observed in the rebuilding of Chicago after the disastrous fire of 1871. The spirit of the New Chicago is well stated by a contemporary.

> Today (1883) Chicago counts her great fire as one of her chief blessings. The city is entirely rebuilt, but not with rickety wooden structures, the previous plentitude of which had rendered her so easy a prey to the devouring element. Solid, substantial, handsome, and in many instances magnificent, the stranger can scarcely realize that these

blocks of buildings are not the growth of a century, or of a generation even, but have sprung from the ground almost in a night. The new Chicago is surprisingly beautiful and grand. The visitor will walk through squares of streets, each teeming with life and commercial activity, and bearing no trace, save in increased elegance, of the disaster of little more than a decade ago; and if forced to the conclusion that, for courage and enterprise, Chicago has proved herself unsurpassed by any city in the world.

Chicago has a major frontage of thirty-eight miles, of which twenty-four are improved, without including the lake front, where an outer harbor is in process of construction. The rivers are now spanned by thirty-five drawbridges, while a tunnel, 16.8 feet long, with a descent of forty-five feet, connects the south and west sides of Washington street, and another tunnel, with a total length of 1,854 feet, connects the north and south sides on the line of LaSalle Street.

State Street, on the southside, is the Broadway of Chicago. Randolph Street is famous for its magnificent buildings, among which are the city and the county halls. . . . The Chamber of Commerce, a spacious and imposing building, with elaborate interior decorations, is at the corner of Washington and LaSalle Streets, opposite City Hall Square, its ceiling is frescoed with allegorical pictures representing the trade of the city, the great fire and the rebuilding. . . .

Among the hotels of Chicago the Palmer House takes the head. This house was destroyed by the fire, but has been rebuilt with a magnitude and elaborateness far exceeding its former self, and constituting it one of the finest, if not the finest in the world. It is entirely fireproof, being constructed only of incombustible materials, brick, stone, iron, marble and cement. It has three fronts, on State and Monroe Streets and Wabash Avenue, and the building and furnishing cost $3,500,000. . . . There are almost three hundred churches in Chicago, including those untouched by fire and those which have since rebuilt. The Great Tabernacle, on Monroe Street, where Messrs. Moody and Sankey held their meetings, is used for sacred concerts and other religious gatherings, and will seat a thousand persons.

In literary and educational institutions Chicago holds a

foremost place. Its common schools are among the best in the country, with large, handsome, convenient and well-ventilated buildings. The University of Chicago, founded by the late Stephen A. Douglas, occupies the largest telescope in America. . . . There are three theological seminaries, and three medical colleges, three hospitals, and a large number of charitable institutions within the city. The fire department is most efficiently organized, and its annual expenses are scarcely less than $1,000,000.

Chicago has the most extensive system of parks and boulevards of any city in the United States. Lincoln Park, lying upon the lake to the northward, contains 310 acres. . . . Humboldt Park, Central Park, and Douglas Park extend along the western boundaries of the city, are large, contain lakes, ponds, walks, drives, fountains and statuary, and are connected with each other by wide and elaborately orna-mented boulevards. . . .

(Chicago) is today increasing its population, developing its resources, and extending its commercial enterprises to a degree that is scarcely credible, save as one is faced by actual facts and figures. There are miles of streets, filled with the incessant roar of business; there lofty temples, magnificent warehouses and elegant residences; there public institutions and learning; this gigantic commerce, this high degree of civilization; all of which have been attained by older cities after a prolonged struggle with adversity, are here the creations and accumulations of less than two generations. Up the Chicago River, where considerably less than a century ago, the Indian paddled his solitary canoe, and John Jacob Astor annually sent his single small schooner to bring provisions to the garrison and take away his furs, there a fleet of vessels of all descriptions, bringing goods from, and sending them to every quarter of the world.*

The characteristics of this new Chicago were common to the majority of our Midwestern cities. The hub of each metropolis was the thriving downtown. This new core, never

---

* Willard Glazier, *Peculiarities of American Cities*, Philadelphia, 1883, pp. 168-75.

easily defined, naturally varied from city to city. In some cities, boundaries were fixed by transportation facilities. The loop in Chicago is a curious example of the informal establishment of a business district bounded by the streets where the elevated lines literally went around a loop. The Loop in Chicago is also an illustration of an area which was adjacent to the railroads. Interesting and colorful names were given to the downtown of major areas of other cities.

Many were attracted daily to the downtown because of the superior shopping facilities. The department stores were the chief attraction. Usually these emporiums catered to customers desiring quality goods. Innumerable specialty stores supplemented the resources of the department stores.

Commerce was also centered in the downtown house zone. An ever increasing number of skyscrapers housed professional people and commercial agents.

Cities had wholesale centers usually adjacent to water or railroad terminals. Wholesale houses enlarged their inventories to serve the growing number of retailers. By the beginning of this century we had placed less dependence upon the old-fashioned market.

A great deal of economic activity was, of course, evident on all of the business streets. The proper choice of a location was important for the successful businessman. Neighborhood shopping centers manifested their share in the economic hustle and bustle of the cities.

New trends in Midwestern urbanization were not confined to the physical. Our cities met successfully a host of new problems. Trained fire departments, with new equipment, replaced old volunteer fire-fighters. We trained more modern and more efficient police departments to cope with many urban problems. Our cities consulted engineering experts and medical experts in the planning of sanitation systems and water kept pace with the population growth.

City governments were also influenced by the new humanitarian trends. More liberal appropriations and better administration assured a more efficient operation of the growing number of urban-operated charitable institutions. Both the contributions of philanthropists and public sums were spent to alleviate at least some of the effects of poverty —a misfortune in an urban age.

Private charity at first was closely identified with religion. The majority of denominations established homes for the orphans and the aged. Great impetus to charity should be credited to the Roman Catholic Church. The orders devoted to charity were able to "step in" rapidly to establish the much needed institutions. The Sisters of Charity, by way of illustration, in 1846 founded Detroit's first hospital, St. Mary's, at the request of Bishop Peter LeFevre. By 1896 Catholic orders had established four hospitals in Chicago. Many Catholic charities rendered non-sectarian services.

In the eighteen eighties the Salvation Army began its programs of social services in many of the cities. It was especially skilled in recognizing the peculiar character of urban problems. By 1900 it was only one of the many Catholic, Protestant, and Jewish church organizations concerned with the social problems of the city.

In the meantime charitable organizations, without any denominational basis or affiliation, became important. Often these groups sponsored only one event such as a Christmas gift box for each youngster in a family without means. Others, such as the free legal aid agencies, were active throughout the entire year. After World War I, in many cities, the drives for these charities were consolidated as the Community Chest.

Public welfare in cities goes back to a very early time when supervisors made appropriations for the poor. These provisions to aid the needy covered even some temporary indigents who were victims of depressions. Relief under these circumstances, however, was ordinarily limited to a few weeks and not intended as a general unemployment expedient. Many were unwilling to apply for assistance because of the stigma attached to welfare. The Great Depression of the thirties resulted in an enlargement of relief programs and a relaxation of policies. Thousands of recipients were temporarily unemployed and not paupers in the older sense of the term. Assistance to a portion of the needy continued even after New Deal policies shifted the general responsibility to the federal government. City assistance is now given primarily to unemployables.

Cities, in spite of the charge of impersonality, have civic pride. Each Midwestern city has its own identity. No city ever attempted to imitate the cities of the East. Some of our Midwestern cities emphasized reform. Others boasted that they were not ready for reform. Yet, at an early time in our history cities were proud of their achievements. One of the first evidences of this pride was the establishment of parks. These parks ordinarily were created in downtown locations. The acreage was insignificant in comparison with the huge recreational centers of this century. Yet, these early parks were oases in the often otherwise drab business areas.

The emphasis upon an attractive physical appearance has been most noticeable in this century. In addition to an elaborate parks program, cities have become conscious of zoning. Early building permits often assured a minimum safety. Ultimately cities would not issue building permits, especially in residential sections, unless specifications conformed to neighborhood goals. Out of these steps grew a zoning plan outlined by city planners.

City planners, of whom many are engineers and architects, began to think in terms of other than business and residential areas. They came to envision cultural centers. Highway planning included not only steps to care for an ever increasing traffic plan, but also for parkways. No amount of planning can serve as an aesthetic substitute for beautiful countryside. Nevertheless many city parkways conform to the highest artistic standards.

Urban redevelopment is a recent term. The phrase was used often to refer to the slum clearance program of the nineteen thirties. By the middle of the century urban redevelopment had come to include steps for middle-class housing (most often financed by private capital), low cost public housing, and even newly planned business areas. In other words city governments, themselves, stepped in to prevent blight.

Civic pride is reflected in athletics. Professional baseball became popular in the eighteen eighties. Late in that decade the Chicago White Stockings played to large crowds. The popularity of the team could be partially attributed to the leadership of the colorful Adrian (Cap) Anson. Contemporary Chicago fans, of course, follow the fortunes of the South Side "White Sox" or North Side "Cubs." In the early nineteen twenties, Tris Speaker of the Cleveland Indians and Tyrus (Ty) Cobb of the Detroit Tigers were almost heroes in their respective cities. Thousands of individuals, some of whom have little other identification with their city, identify themselves closely with one of the baseball or other professional athletic teams.

The increase in population of the Midwestern cities has resulted from a migration from our rural areas and a particular appeal for the European immigrant. In 1890 every geographic area in the United States was represented among the native-born population of Chicago. Some forty-six per cent of the native-born population claimed the states of the old Northwest as their place of birth; five per cent were born in the Middle Atlantic states; three per cent were born in New England; two per cent were born in the new trans-Mississippi West.

In 1890 over forty per cent of the Chicago population was foreign born. This abnormally high percentage speaks well for the opportunities found in the city. Of the immigrants the largest number, thirty-seven per cent, were born in the German States. Approximately twenty-four per cent were born in the British Isles; five per cent were born in Bohemia; five per cent were born in Russia; fifteen per cent were born in Scandinavia; and six per cent in Canada.

A favorable social climate awaited the immigrant in the city. Here he could live with people who spoke his tongue and knew his ways. If the colony were large enough, it virtually constituted a city within a city. In many respects the adjustment of the immigrant to the city was less difficult than it was for many of the rural native-born.

The official population of a city listed by the Census Bureau is no longer the index of size. By 1930, the Census Bureau recognized official metropolitan districts. Each of these metropolitan areas consisted of a city and the towns that had grown up beyond its town limits. Although each of the suburbs had its own local government, the majority of the inhabitants were also closely identified with the larger city. Governmental cooperation among all of the units was necessary to assure adequate programs of such services as transportation and water supply. Gradually, many came to realize that the new urbanization was creating problems best handled by some type of metropolitan action.

In 1960 four of the twelve largest metropolitan areas were in the Middle West. The Chicago area ranked third in the nation with a population of 6,176,000. The Detroit area, with 3,743,000 inhabitants, was fifth. The eleventh place was held by the Cleveland area with a population of 1,786,000. The Minneapolis area ranked twelfth with a population of 1,474,000. Interestingly, in 1960, Midwesterners were reading about the "400-mile city" of the not-too-distant future, running from Milwaukee to Detroit and encompassing Milwaukee, Chicago, and the intermediate cities between Chicago and Detroit.

Some Reading Aids

BOND, BEVERLEY. *The Civilization of the Old Northwest.* New York, 1934.

BULEY, ROSCOE. *The Old Northwest.* 2 vols. Indianapolis, 1950.

FOX, DIXON RYAN (Ed.). *Sources of Culture in the Middle West.* New York, 1934.

GARLAND, JOHN (Ed.). *The North American Midwest: A Regional Geography,* New York, 1955.

HAVIGHURST, WALTER. *Land of the Long Horizon.* New York, 1960.

————. *Land of Promise,* New York, 1946.

HUTTON, GRAHAM. *Midwest at Noon.* Chicago, 1946.

MC AVOY, THOMAS. *The Midwest: Myth or Reality.* South Bend, Indiana, 1961.

MURRAY, JOHN (Ed.). *The Heritage of the Middle West.* Norman, Oklahoma, 1958.

NYE, RUSSEL. *Midwestern Progressive Politics.* East Lansing, Michigan, 1959.

OGG, FREDERIC. *The Old Northwest,* New Haven, Connecticut, 1919.

Index